Seamus Heaney

Open Guides to Literature

Series Editor: Graham Martin (Professor of Literature, The Open University)

Titles in the Series

Angus Calder: Byron
Jenni Calder: *Animal Farm* and *1984*
Walford Davies: Dylan Thomas
Roger Day: Larkin
Peter Faulkner: Yeats
Anthony Fothergill: *Heart of Darkness*
P. N. Furbank: Pound
Brean Hammond: *Gulliver's Travels*
Graham Holderness: *Hamlet*
Graham Holderness: *Women in Love*
Graham Holderness: *Wuthering Heights*
Jeannette King: *Jane Eyre*
Graham Martin: *Great Expectations*
David B. Pirie: Shelley
Jeremy Tambling: What is Literary Language?
Ronald Tamplin: Seamus Heaney
Dennis Walder: Ted Hughes
Roderick Watson: MacDiarmid
Ruth Whittaker: *Tristram Shandy*

Seamus Heaney
(courtesy of Faber and Faber)

RONALD TAMPLIN

Seamus Heaney

Open University Press
Milton Keynes · Philadelphia

Open University Press
12 Cofferidge Close
Stony Stratford
Milton Keynes MK11 1BY

and
1900 Frost Road, Suite 101
Bristol, PA 19007, USA

First Published 1989

British Library Cataloguing in Publication Data

Tamplin, Ronald
Seamus Heaney. – (Open guides to literature)
1. Poetry in English. Heaney, Seamus, 1939– critical studies
I. Title
821′.914

ISBN 0-335-15262-7
ISBN 0-335-15261-9

Library of Congress Cataloging-in-Publication Data available

Typeset by Rowland Phototypesetting Limited,
Bury St Edmunds, Suffolk
Printed in Great Britain by
J. W. Arrowsmith Limited, Bristol

For Anne, Mary,
Peter and Clare

Contents

Series Editor's Preface		x
Acknowledgements		xii
1	Introduction	1
2	Nature, History, Darkness	14
3	Image, Language, Distance	34
4	*North*	51
5	*Field Work*	72
6	*Station Island* and After	88
Notes		103
Suggestions for Further Reading		109
Index		111

Series Editor's Preface

The intention of this series is to provide short introductory books about major writers, texts, and literary concepts for students of courses in Higher Education which substantially or wholly involve the study of Literature.

The series adopts a pedagogic approach and style similar to that of Open University material for Literature courses. *Open Guides* aim to inculcate the reading 'skills' which many introductory books in the field tend, mistakenly, to assume that the reader already possesses. They are, in this sense, 'teacherly' texts, planned and written in a manner which will develop in the reader the confidence to undertake further independent study of the topic. They are 'open' in two senses. First, they offer a three-way tutorial exchange between the writer of the *Guide*, the text or texts in question, and the reader. They invite readers to join in an exploratory discussion of texts, concentrating on their key aspects and on the main problems which readers, coming to the texts for the first time, are likely to encounter. The flow of a *Guide* 'discourse' is established by putting questions for the reader to follow up in a tentative and searching spirit, guided by the writer's comments, but not dominated by an over-arching and single-mindedly-pursued argument or evaluation, which itself requires to be 'read'.

Guides are also 'open' in a second sense. They assume that literary texts are 'plural', that there is no end to interpretation, and that it is for the reader to undertake the pleasurable task of discovering meaning and value in such texts. *Guides* seek to provide, in compact form, such relevant biographical, historical and cultural information as bears upon the reading of the text, and they point the reader to a selection of the best available critical discussions of it. They are not in themselves concerned to propose, or to counter, particular readings of the texts, but rather to put *Guide* readers in a position to do that for themselves. Experienced travellers learn to dispense with guides, and so it should be for readers of this series.

This *Open Guide* to the poetry of Seamus Heaney is best studied in conjunction with *Seamus Heaney. Selected Poems 1965–75* published by Faber and Faber (London, 1980). Page references in the *Guide* are to this edition. *The Penguin Book of Contemporary British Poetry* (Blake Morrison and Andrew Motion eds) published by Penguin Books (London, 1982) will also be helpful.

Graham Martin

Acknowledgements

I would like to thank Anthony Fothergill, Peter Faulkner, Graham Martin, Michael Wood and my students over the years for particular help in the matter of Heaney. And of course my family to whom this book is dedicated.

Author and publisher are grateful for the following permissions to reprint copyright material: from (a) *The Haw Lantern* (b) *Death of a Naturalist* (c) *Field Work* (d) *Door into the Dark* and further materials from *Wintering Out*, *North*, *Station Island*, *Preoccupations: Selected Prose 1968–1978* and *The Government of the Tongue*, all by Seamus Heaney and reprinted by permission of Faber and Faber Ltd./Farrar Straus & Giroux; from T. S. Eliot, *Collected Poems 1909–1962* by permission of Faber and Faber Ltd./Harcourt Brace Jovanovich; from Grahame Greene, *The Ministry of Fear* by permission of William Heinemann Ltd., The Bodley Head Ltd./ Viking Penguin; from Patrick Kavanagh, *The Complete Poems* and *Lough Derg* by permission of The Goldsmith Press Ltd., Newbridge, County Kildare; from Philip Larkin, *The Whitsun Weddings* by permission of Faber and Faber Ltd.; from Sean O'Faolain, 'Lovers of the Lake', in *Stories of Sean O'Faolain* by permission of A. P. Watt Ltd./Curtis Brown Ltd. on behalf of Sean O'Faolain; from W. B. Yeats, *The Collected Poems*, *Autobiographies* and the preface to *Oxford Book of Modern Verse* (1936) by permission of A. P. Watt Ltd. on behalf of Michael B. Yeats and Macmillan London Ltd./ Macmillan Publishing Company Inc.; from James Carney, *Medieval Irish Lyrics* (1967); from Georges Charbonnier, *Conversations with Claude Lévi-Strauss* by permission of Jonathan Cape Ltd.; from Neil Corcoran, *Seamus Heaney* by permission of Faber and Faber Ltd.; from Polly Devlin, *all of us there* (Weidenfeld and Nicolson) by permission of the author and Marie Heaney; from Edna Longley, *Poetry in the Wars* (Bloodaxe Books, 1986 and Associated University Presses, 1987) by permission of Bloodaxe Books/Associated University Presses; from Blake Morrison, *Seamus Heaney* by permission of Methuen & Co. Ltd. and the author; from Blake Morrison in *British Poetry since 1970* by permission of Carcanet Press Ltd. and the author; from Cecil Woodham-Smith, *The Great Hunger* by permission of Hamish Hamilton Ltd.

Photographs: Seamus Heaney, by courtesy of Faber and Faber Ltd.; Tollund Man from P. V. Glob, *The Bog People*, reprinted by permission of Faber and Faber Ltd.; Gallarus Oratory, courtesy of Bord Failte, photograph by Paddy Tutty; Newgrange by permission of the Commissioner of Public Works, Ireland.

1. Introduction

Seamus Heaney was born in 1939 at Mossbawn in the townland of Tamniarn near Bellaghy in County Derry, Northern Ireland, the eldest child in a farming family. Since 1966, when his first book, *Death of a Naturalist*, was published, his reputation as a poet has gone from strength to strength. And it is not a matter alone of reputation. There are few poets now writing in these islands whose work consistently matches Heaney's in its importance and quality. In many ways he is not an innovative poet. He has not recast radically the habitual language of poetry. He has not challenged our preconceptions with a new poetic form nor has he led us into the recognition of new rhythms and metres. Instead he has worked with what was to hand and brought to it great powers of expression and art as well as a significant subject matter. He is, eminently, a readable poet here and now and one who needs to be read.

This brief book is about reading his poetry and, by way of that, in a wider sense, about reading any poetry. Reading poetry is reading poems and that's what we will be doing. Fully to read a poem we sometimes need to be clearly aware of its contexts, both of time and place. I will fill in some of these contexts as we go through. The first, and the most vital to keep in mind, is that Heaney is an Irish poet, but a special kind of Irish poet. He is born in what is, politically speaking, Northern Ireland, part of the United Kingdom. Geographically speaking, we can call this the North of Ireland – which may be to make a very different kind of statement, at once geographical and political, even – one can hazard the word – spiritual. His people were Catholics, the majority religion in the whole island of Ireland but a minority in the Protestant and Unionist North. They were Nationalist, as Catholics mostly are, but passive rather than active politically. To be absolutely explicit, Heaney is not a special kind of English poet, but an Irish poet who writes in English. We will come back to this assertion and look at it more thoroughly.

To begin at the beginning, I would like you to read the poem

'Digging' (*Selected Poems*, p. 10). This is the poem that opens Heaney's first book, *Death of a Naturalist*. In that sense it opens a career. We could think of it as a manifesto or a statement of intent. When you have read it through a couple of times, to give shape to our discussion, you could first formulate a rough and literal statement of what the poem seems to say. When I say 'literal' I mean just that. Initially, don't think about abstracts and symbols so much as concrete statement. Don't think about 'Love', but of the actions by which we recognize love, or more to the point here, not 'Work' with a capital letter, but some action which is a type of work. And after you have got this first rough statement, clarify it by asking yourself a few questions. What does the writer's father dig up for us to discover? What contrasts does Heaney make between himself, on the one hand, and his father and grandfather on the other? Is the poem about a break with the past or a continuity with it? Do you think the poem is at all about the nature of work? The best way into a poem and its distinctive statement is through the words, what sorts of words they are and how they are used. I mean by that, don't strain after things to say about rhyme-schemes or rhythms even, though these may seem to be the things that make the statement before you a poem rather than any other kind of statement. And so, lastly, a question about one of the words here. What do you make of the image in the second line which describes the writer's pen resting between finger and thumb, 'snug as a gun'?

DISCUSSION

Let's see how this might turn out.

This is not a complex poem. But it has some startling features. The poem begins with Heaney writing, pen in hand. Under the window, his father digs the garden ('flowerbeds'), reminding Heaney how his father and, twenty years before that, his grandfather had dug potatoes and turf, with craftlike perfection. Turf is what in England is called 'peat'. It is used for fuel. Heaney can't handle a spade like that, but he'll dig with the pen.

Heaney then seems to be observing a break with the past. Of the three men in the poem, grandfather, father and son, it is the son who is the odd man out. 'But I've no spade to follow men like them.' Nonetheless he asserts a continuity, in that the action of digging, which is the running image throughout the poem ('My father, digging . . . where he was digging . . .'), is identical with Heaney's own future use for his pen. 'I'll dig with it.' Poetry will be used as a means of revealing, ('buried the bright edge deep / To scatter new potatoes.') The potatoes, which his father's digging had revealed, were objects of perfection and regard, much as poems are. ('Loving their cool hardness in our hands'.) So too digging means going beyond the ordinary surfaces ('down and down / For the good turf'), just as poems are meant to go beyond surfaces. The 'cuts of an edge / Through living roots' awaken in Heaney's mind roots at once living and in process of severance. The memories and the traditions impel Heaney to see his own poetic vocation as one more man digging. Throughout the poem words and images are applied to digging which suggest its qualities as craft and its associated techniques: '*clean* rasping sound', 'Stooping in *rhythm*', 'nestled on the lug', 'levered firmly', 'bright edge', 'Nicking and slicing neatly'. There is no sense that the pen is mightier than the spade. Indeed the reverse. The sedentary habits of the poet are hinted at. Heaney is withdrawn from the action, even from the activeness of his father's old age in the garden. Instead he is inside the window, looking on. The pen is 'squat' as opposed to the almost elegant words applied to the spade and its uses. The poet is seen in memory as a child who once carried to his grandfather milk in a bottle. The bottle is 'corked sloppily' and this contrasts with the grandfather's firmness and vigour of body. ('He straightened up / To drink it, then fell to right away / Nicking and slicing neatly'). But, at the same time, since the pen too will be used 'to dig', all the craft-qualities of digging apply to the poetic vocation. And so continuity in difference is asserted.

Why is Heaney at such pains to assert such continuity? Two other attitudes often prevail in writing about this crucial moment of realization when the child diverges in its ways or social station from the parent. One is nostalgia for an irrecoverable past. The other, exemplified by the endings of D. H. Lawrence's *Sons and Lovers* and James Joyce's *Portrait of the Artist as a Young Man*, is a more or less thrusting assertion, a break. Significantly both these books are about artists emergent, and the key image is of travel from the childhood locale to the big city or abroad. And the heroism is firmly located in the defiant artist figures Paul Morel and Stephen Dedalus. In 'Digging' no such break occurs. As an artist, he will still be digging. The milieu will remain intact and he will still be within it. And he will be hero only as part of an ancestral heroism:

> My grandfather cut more turf in a day
> Than any other man on Toner's bog.

Where Lawrence and Joyce are individualist and assertive, Heaney is social and effaces himself within a tradition and indeed a locale. 'Toner's bog', unknown to us otherwise, is the scene of genuinely heroic endeavour, in which work measures heroic satisfaction and is not just a means of getting on, of aggrandizement. This heroic theme, oddly enough, has not often expressed itself in English writing. Manual work itself is not frequently celebrated in English poetry. Is it because English society had tended to associate manual work with the despised 'hewers of wood and drawers of water'? (*Joshua* 9.21)

To find work treated as heroic activity the closest and most apt parallel is in Ireland, with Patrick Kavanagh. Kavanagh (1904–1967) is an Irish poet who has some similarities with Heaney. He was born in Mucker, County Monaghan. His father was a cobbler and small farmer. He began writing in the late 1920s and later moved to Dublin, leading an impoverished and somewhat tetchy literary life. He is a fine lyric poet. *The Great Hunger* (1942) is his major poem. His autobiographical novels *The Green Fool* (1938) and *Tarry Flynn* (1948), depicting Irish rural life, are well worth reading. His importance is more thoroughly recognized in Ireland than in England. In a penetrating essay 'From Monaghan to the Grand Canal' Heaney speaks of him 'raising the inhibited energies of a subculture to the power of a cultural resource'.[1] Heaney's tone and use of locale are close to Kavanagh's poem 'Epic'.

> I have lived in important places, times
> When great events were decided, who owned
> That half a rood of rock, a no-man's land
> Surrounded by our pitchfork-armed claims.
> I heard the Duffys shouting 'Damn your soul'
> And old McCabe stripped to the waist, seen
> Step the plot defying blue cast-steel –
> 'Here is the march along these iron stones'
> That was the year of the Munich bother. Which
> Was more important? I inclined
> To lose my faith in Ballyrush and Gortin
> Till Homer's ghost came whispering to my mind
> He said: I made the Iliad from such
> A local row. Gods make their own importance.[2]

The world Kavanagh celebrates fits well with Heaney's poem. Is it too facile to suggest that some at least of Heaney's need to establish such continuity is implicit in his situation, Catholic Nationalist in the Unionist North? Roots are the means to prolong life. An heroic past allows the possibility of an heroic future. Allied to this is another concern of the poem, an attempt to locate an identity. He resists deracination and uses the household gods of the Irish land – turf, fuel, for light, heat and hearth, and the potato, food and sullen betrayer – to name himself. As to that image I asked you to consider – 'The squat pen rests; snug as a gun' – in the Irish context it must at least have overtones of the intimate association between the gun and politics and the gun and literature. The university student's choice in the old revolutionary Ireland earlier in the century was between the gun, the books and the bottle, so the image has sinister possibilities hardly to be expected in an English poem (unless actually about war). In an Irish one, it is disturbing but not out of place.

We can also refer to Heaney's essay 'Feeling into Words', originally given as a lecture at the Royal Society of Literature in 1974.[3] In it, Heaney examines the origins of his early poems and he sees poetry 'as divination, poetry as revelation of the self to the self, as restoration of the culture to itself'.[4] From some interesting comments on 'Digging' I want to select just one phrase which seems to me very helpful in estimating the way a poem works. He speaks of his poem as 'an enactment of . . . [a] digging metaphor'.[5] It is as if the poet latches on to some ancestral or communal usage, a proverb, a cliché even, which we all have in our minds and have got used to, and then teases out of it further skeins of meaning. The poem 'enacts' that process of exploration. And, of course for us, reading and analysing the poem continues that process and we participate in it with the poet. We need not necessarily reach all the way the poet does or we may even get different satisfactions and meanings from our own 'enactment'. So long as we remain in the rough field of the poem's energies our reading will be good, because we too respond to the ranges of the original metaphor that the poem has directed us to. Poems then, however carefully they are made, are not concerned simply with exact communication, but rather direct us to thought which cannot quite be specified.

The next poem I want you to look at is 'Bogland' (pp. 53–4), the last poem in his second book *Door into the Dark* (1969). Heaney is very careful about first and last poems, as if he is throwing you into his book with the first and directing you on, to whatever is to come next time out, with the last. Read the poem a couple of times and rough out what it says. Again don't be afraid to be very simple and basic in what you say. 'Digging' had locatable human figures – the writer, the father, the grandfather. Can you locate figures in 'Bogland'? How are they referred to? By name? Who do you think 'we' are, in the first line? Is this a poem about a particular type of landscape? Or a particular psychology, even a spirit? Look at those images the 'sun' and the 'eye' in stanzas one and two, the 'bog' in stanza two and the 'Great Irish Elk' in stanza three. Do you get a sense of expansion or contraction from them or could you get both of those senses at once? The images of the elk, the ground, thought of as butter, and the trunks of firs have an element in common. What is it? Can we speak of the past and the present in the last five stanzas? If we can, how do past and present relate to one another? Just as we picked up on an odd phrase, 'snug as a gun', in 'Digging', what do you make of the word 'kind' to describe 'ground' and 'butter'? What does it mean, do you think? The last line of the poem is 'The wet centre is bottomless'. Does this seem to you a negative or affirmative thing to say about the bogland? Could you answer that both ways?

DISCUSSION

The poem is an account of the boglands that form the geological base of much of Ireland. In Ireland there are no prairies. The effect of the landscape is to narrow the gaze 'into the cyclops' eye / Of a tarn'. It preserves things from the past, the now extinct but enormous Great Irish Elk, hundred-year old butter, great firs. The ground is itself pliable as butter: it will never be coal. The pioneers of this country dig down and down, meeting evidences of previous occupancy. 'The wet centre is bottomless.'

'Bogland' has, perhaps appropriately then, a less perceptible centre than 'Digging'. The human figures, so strong in 'Digging', are generalized to pronouns. 'We', 'our', 'they've', 'they'll'. Actions are impersonalized, 'the eye concedes', 'is wooed', 'butter . . . was recovered . . .'. The effect is to widen the number of people that the poem refers to. In 'Digging' the tradition is visible in three people. In 'Bogland', 'we' is coextensive with all the inhabitants past, present and future of Ireland. The poem claims them all as subject to the same conditions; geographical conditions, bog as compared with prairie; psychological conditions, perhaps metaphysical, certainly of the spirit. The first two stanzas are all to do with expansions and contractions of the horizon. The prairie spreads vision outward, to slice the sun. The bogland draws the eye in, the horizon encroaches on it and vision is narrowed into the small lake, like the cyclops' one eye. This is to be understood probably less as a narrowing than as a concentration and this concentrating is the product of love. The eye is wooed. The country is 'ours' and 'unfenced'. The bog is still in growth, in renewal, 'crusting' and accreting as it comes under the fire of the sun, 'between the sights of the sun'. Much as in 'Digging', Heaney is here accepting what some might see as limited conditions as a necessary definition allowing growth.

Furthermore the bog preserves the past, enabling it to impact sensationally on the present. The Great Irish Elk, *Megacerous Hibernicus*, which had antlers thirteen feet across, the largest of any known deer, 'an astounding crate full of air', is a note of expansion in the poem, but still, in 'crate', given defining limits. Heaney is here establishing a continuity from past to present, in the natural world. The bog is the medium through which that continuity is established. Butter, preserved good a hundred years, forms a continuity in the domestic world and also becomes a metaphor for the ground itself. Again there is a note of expansion, 'the ground' is 'kind' black butter.

'Kind' here has a range of meaning. There is an affirmative vision of a 'kind' land nurturing its people, perhaps, of kinship. But there is more to it than that. It melts and opens underfoot. The movement it invites is downwards, just as the eye, in the first two stanzas, was not wooed outwards but inwards into the eye of the tarn. And just as in 'Digging' Heaney's grandfather went down and down for the good turf. Such earth cannot be defined and so limited. Its meaning is, in that sense, infinite and so, at first sight, what seems an imprecision, in that we would require solidity of the land we walk on, becomes its virtue. It resists definition, finality. Peat will not here form coal, hard rock. In Ireland one might easily, in the face of English puzzlement at the virtues of turf as fuel, identify England with its product coal, in the wake of Swift's advice to burn everything English except their coal.[6] From the deep ground only the trunks of firs surface, great as the elk, born of a past heroic world. Ireland's pioneers follow the dominant movement of the poem, inwards and downwards, and as they lay bare the land, find again ancestral continuities, connect with the massive offshore sea, the Atlantic, and reach to a bottomless wet centre. The poem's affirmation is conducted through an unusual set of images in which going inwards and downwards towards a bottomless wet pit are positive terms. The taut presentation of this poem has made the image of turf as it appears in 'Digging' into something like a metaphysical ground of being – bog as origin and total expression. Bottomless equals infinite. Wet centre implies fecundity. T. E. Hulme, the English philosopher and imagist poet, who died in the First World War, said that he first understood the meaning of God on the Canadian prairies.[7] Heaney sees a similar infinity in a completely contrary landscape. 'Bogland' constructs a myth of the bog. The natural form is used to carry a large symbolic meaning. And it will be a key symbol for Heaney. Ireland has an impressively coherent and elaborate mythology, and in the restoring of the national consciousness in the nineteenth and early twentieth centuries, that mythology played a key role as scholars recovered, edited and translated the early texts, and poets popularized and dramatized them. Yeats employed this mythology. But Heaney, at this stage in his writing, does not. Instead he uses natural forms and archaeology to establish his all-encompassing myths.

In each of the two poems we have looked at, 'Digging' and 'Bogland', a unity has been implied, though in each a certain toughness of mind might have been required for the unity to be established. In the first a unity was forged between Heaney and the Irish familial traditions he sees as ancestrally his. In the second, an opposition prairie / bogland is manufactured rather than implicit. Why should the prairie be there at all in the poem, except to say that it has nothing to do with the Irish at home in the bogland? From then on, the poem is all about the coming together, the melting into one of its various components. The opposing functions, 'big sun' and 'coal', are, as it were, outside the onward, or rather downward, movements of the poem, stalking horses only. There is, I think, a subtler and more ingenious opposition implied though. Heaney constantly takes negative-looking or unpleasing properties and embraces them as something to be celebrated: 'encroaching', 'cyclops' eye', 'crusting', 'sunk under', 'missing . . . definition', 'soft as pulp', 'inwards', 'downwards', 'seepage', 'wet centre', 'bottomless'. It is Ireland's peculiar quality to divine virtue in the apparently unrewarding, to secure it in the neglected. We can return to this, but at this point it would be worth bearing in mind the negative affirmation in the title of the book in which 'Bogland' appears, *Door into the Dark*, where the dark becomes revelatory not restrictive.

Heaney's essay 'Feeling into Words' also includes an account of 'Bogland', explaining how he came to introduce the prairie into it.

> At that time I was teaching modern literature in Queen's University, Belfast, and had been reading about the frontier and the west as an important myth in the American consciousness, so I set up – or rather, laid down – the bog as an answering Irish myth.[8]

This is nice, not so much because it explains what might otherwise seem a gratuitous comparison, but because it lets us into the workings of a poet's mind. For Heaney, at that moment, there was no discontinuity between his natural observation of the boglands and his reading. And, of course, he need not, in fact, have seen, say, ancient butter taken from the bog, or fir trees. He needs only to have heard or read that they had been. In the poet's mind, as in everybody's, observation and reading, nature and literature are all potent. Reading is only another sort of observation. When that reading is in other poets we will talk of echoes and influences and so on but what we are really seeing is a sort of mutuality among the writers, an interdependence which we can call a tradition. In this particular case the reference is not specific to any particular writer but to many American usages, in such poets as Walt Whitman or in Westerns. Later though we will come across deliberate and relished echoes or references in Heaney, to his predecessors and mentors. It is another means to locate his own nature.

Did you notice that 'Bogland' is much more tightly expressed than 'Digging'? There is an expansiveness of description in 'Digging' which Heaney does not allow himself in the taut oppositions and parallels of his four-line 'Bogland' stanzas. And when he does let himself go with an effect it is fruitful, as with 'encroaching horizon', a phrase that encapsulates much of the apparent paradox of the poem. The comparison in 'Digging' is with 'curt cuts', which indicates a similar playfulness in handling language but is a bit tricksy, even disruptive. We might want to see this tightness as 'development', but I don't think so. It is rather a question of the needs of the poem. We see in Heaney a full range in action rather than a sequence of manners.

Now let's look at 'The Other Side' (pp. 71–3), a poem from Heaney's next book, *Wintering Out* (1972). This time try reading the poem aloud. It has a lot of voice – indeed voices – in it. In poems, things which don't seem so clear often unravel as you speak. And the rhythms of the words are not always easy to realize just by reading in the mind.

And following the comparison of 'Bogland' with 'Digging', we could start with a different question. How is this poem written? Tightly or loosely? Is it more like 'Bogland' or 'Digging'? Look over the three of them together and see what you think. I have tried to suggest that 'Digging' and 'Bogland' each establish some idea of unity in their thought. Is there such a unity in 'The Other Side'? What is the other side? What, then, is the opening speaker's own side? And, to make a jump, is this a poem about politics? Or religion? Or about neighbours? These questions are larger, less pernickety than the ones we have been asking so far, but as before start by reading the poem a couple of times then roughly sketch out a prose meaning. Pursue the questions I have suggested. Don't let the general terms 'political' or 'religious' drive you off from a particularity in your answers. For example, do you think the farmer would like the things Heaney is saying about him? Can you 'hear' the farmer speaking? Is he an heroic figure? Does his language have a particular flavour? Or, another way of looking at that, does he use a particular set of words? Who is the observer in the poem? Is there more than one observer? Is there a change of age in the observer or observers? Why do you think Heaney says 'a' neighbour instead of 'our' neighbour in the second line? Suppose Heaney had written 'the' chosen people or 'a' chosen people in line 12, would it have made any difference other than to the rhythm? Is there a contrast between the kinds of words, taken from the language of religion and used to describe the farmer or used in his speech, and the words and associations used for the prayers of Heaney's people? Finally, at the end of the poem, are Heaney and the farmer together or apart? And how do you know?

DISCUSSION

I suggested earlier that Heaney's choice of looser or tighter style depends upon the particular poem. 'The Other Side' illustrates this openness to different methods. It is strung out and anecdotal as was 'Digging', but tight and firm in its three-line stanza pattern. One way he achieves the quality of freely moving anecdote is by allowing his stanzas to run over one into another, so that they control the poem visually and separate out its distinct moment and pictures but do not segment it grammatically. And so the syntactic flow is not halted. This is one sort of unity operating over material which is conceived sectionally, both in the stanzas and in the three larger sections or phases of the poem. 'Digging' and 'Bogland' establish unities in a further way through their dominant images. Digging equals writing, and prairie and bogland are geographical expressions both of the infinite and of a national consciousness.

With 'The Other Side', no such unity can be taken for granted, though eventually one is at least wistfully asserted. The poem offers an account of a Protestant farmer, neighbouring the Catholic Heaneys, his relations with them, his stance, his habitual conversation, and ultimately the shy intimacies and respects and common cause that bring or might bring both together. In some ways the poem is an exercise in compassionate politics – a remark which may beg a number of questions. Why do I say politics, rather than religion, for example? Is compassion already missing if we must distinguish between 'sides' in this way? To gauge an answer to this second question it might help to read Robert Frost's celebrated poem about neighbourly division and alliance, 'Mending Wall',[9] and to see where, with Frost or with Heaney, the greater degree of compassion and fellow-feeling lies. There's a lot to this poem of Heaney's, delicacies too casually missed. He shares with another contemporary poet, Charles Causley, an ability to savour and relish diverse character.[10] Though presented as lyric or narrative, the poem reveals a dramatic ability. Its insights really depend on gauging what a person might wish to say or to be said about themselves. It observes and sets down characteristic and therefore favoured speech. The insights then are, even when we laugh at them, compassionate and genial rather than ironic, and the comedy defends rather than savages the character who is observed.

There are two observers in the poem. One is Heaney. He sees the neighbouring farmer in Sections I ('I lay where . . . my ear swallowing') and II and III, where, with his friends, or family 'we would rehearse each patriarchal dictum' and 'hear his step round the gable'. In the last half of Section III we may assume that Heaney is older, a grown man, and able to respond to his neighbour as an equal, not simply from the amused, sometimes awed memories of childhood. ('I lay' as compared with 'But now I stand'). If Heaney's standpoint changes, so does that of the man he observes. He begins as 'a neighbour' not, notice, *our* neighbour. Neighbour is already a biblical word, used to specify the relationship in which, in the Gospels, all people stand to us. The indefinite article enhances the relationship in one way, in that it does not narrow the scope of the word just to those who live on either side of us. At the same time it deliberately withdraws the relationship from intimacy. This 'neighbour' is cast in the heroic mould as he towers above the luxuriant but commercially useless growth of sedge and marigolds that separates the Heaney's marshy fallow 'nested on moss and rushes' from his productive meadow ('lea'). He does not speak simply, but vouches, dismisses, prophesies, all words which stem from or assume authority. And he lays his shadow on the stream, darkness falling across the living, moving waters. It's possible this is a deliberate echo of Yeats's poem 'Easter 1916', where, in a passage which contrasts the fixity of firm, even fanatical purpose, with impermanent but living variety, Yeats says

> A shadow of cloud on the stream
> Changes minute by minute.[11]

Certainly it's a nice echo, for here too, although the image is reversed in its application, the contrast is between the seemingly permanent fixity of the prophesying neighbour and the living variety of marigolds and the nestlike moss and rushes, a contrast between Law and Love. Often enough echoes like this in a poet are not deliberate though, but unconscious and come from the fine-tuning of a mind, sensitive to the poetic medium in which it works.

Similarly, it is natural for the neighbour to lace his talk with parallels and examples drawn from the Bible, mostly from the Old Testament, repository of the Law. It is not without its gentle irony that the one New Testament reference, to the parable of the rich man and Lazarus (*Luke* 16:19–31), identifies the scraggy acres of the Heaneys' land with Lazarus who, when he died, 'was carried away by angels to the bosom of Abraham'. It is gentle irony though, because the neighbour's fine proverbial phrase already carries in it a note of compassion. Nonetheless the leafage is 'shaken' as he speaks with the resonance of the Bible in 'that tongue of chosen people'. I think just saying 'chosen people' throws doubt on who does the choosing. The neighbour is not one of 'the' chosen people, that is to say, the Jews. They were chosen by God. Nor is he part of 'a chosen people' which would imply an outside sanction. Somebody, even if it is not God, has chosen them. Instead the neighbour's people are simply 'chosen', and I suspect this suggests that they are self-sanctioned, the Calvinist 'elect'. They do the choosing, or, rather, assume God has, and they appropriate the 'tongue'. It might point up the implied politics of this to wonder how it was the Catholics came to have 'scraggy acres' anyway? Was it that they chose to live on the marginal lands as an act of indigence? or self-denial? Or how else did they get there, 'tares' their inheritance from the swinging blackthorn?

None of this denies the neighbour his patriarchal magnificence though, 'fabulous', 'promised furrows', the great names 'rolled magnificently like loads of hay'. 'Rolled' is a beautifully poised word in that it refers simultaneously to the rolling words of his speech and to the laden hay-wagons rolling along the neighbour's lanes, 'too big for our small lanes'. The dicta occasionally falter on a rut, his neighbour assuming that all his talk would fall on the deaf ears of a people ignorant of the Bible.

> 'Your side of the house, I believe,
> hardly rule by the book at all.'

Notice the words 'rule' and 'book', with the various usages 'to go by the book', to 'book someone', 'to throw the book at someone', 'the rule of law', and so on, with their inflexibilities. 'Do not all charms fly / At the mere touch of cold philosophy?' asked Keats in his poem *Lamia* where 'all mysteries' are conquered 'by rule and line'.[12] It is a similar contrast that is drawn now by Heaney between the whitewashed, text-hung tidy world and mind of the neighbour and his own family reciting the mysteries of the rosary, a form of popular prayer certainly additional to the Bible but full of feeling and consonant with it. Heaney catches the repetitive manner of the rosary well, 'dragging mournfully on in the kitchen'. Patrick Kavanagh in *The Green Fool* says, 'I am sure that should I ever have an attack of insomnia I need only have somebody start the Rosary and I'm cured',[13] but Sean O'Faolain catches the intention of this prayer form well in his story 'Lovers of the Lake',[14] about a pilgrimage to Lough Derg, the same setting as Heaney will use in his major poem 'Station Island' (1984). He writes

> After that she made a deliberate effort of the mind to mean and to feel every separate word of the prayers – which is a great foolishness since prayers are not poems to be read or even understood; they are an instinct; to dance would be as wise.[15]

But there is another acknowledgement in the neighbour's words. He speaks of 'your side of the house', which suggests there is one house. And as he becomes an observer himself in the remainder of the poem, it is to this side that our attention turns. He waits with courtesy and discretion until the prayers in the Catholic kitchen are over before knocking and casually whistling on the doorstep. He speaks of himself as 'dandering by' – sauntering, very much the off-duty activity – in his true warmth at last. In the next two stanzas he observes and is observed. Himself and Heaney are given that alien intimacy, part voyeur part social worker, that the act of poetry often demands, as they stand, one behind the other 'in the dark yard, in the moan of prayers'. His shy mannerisms and hesitancies, putting his hand in his pocket, tapping 'a little tune' with his blackthorn, formerly the instrument of prophesy, are the diffident respects of the outsider and Heaney compares them to the sense we feel outside others' lovemaking or tears. To get the kindly force of this we could perhaps compare Philip Larkin's outsider's sense in 'The Whitsun Weddings'. At the weddings

> children frowned
> At something dull; fathers had never known
> Success so huge and wholly farcical;
> The women shared
> The secret like a happy funeral;
> While girls, gripping their handbags tighter, stared
> At a religious wounding.[16]

Where Larkin is lonelier, observing exactly a variety of roles but always detached, never quite released from the pains of his own irony, Heaney seems to share his neighbour's courtesy as part of his own. Being outside is not here to be detached. Doubtful and shy as his neighbour, 'Should I slip away' he wonders, or 'touch his shoulder' – the restrained intimacy – and

> talk about the weather
> or the price of grass-seed?

the simple and exact point of contact, the land, the atmospheres of Ireland – their single house. Why is this compassionate politics? Well, for one thing they do not sit down and talk things out, in the mode so beloved of communicators, but cross over the gaps through the concerns of their common humanity. This is in all ways a rich poem.

Let us briefly recapitulate. We have read three of Seamus Heaney's poems, chosen from his first three books. Through them we have examined a number of his themes and contexts: his pursuit of identity and of art ('Digging'); his attempt to locate a specifically Irish national consciousness through the land's habitual landscapes ('Bogland'); and his glimpse of neighbourliness transcending political and religious division in the north of Ireland ('The Other Side'). We have hinted at parallels and comparisons we can helpfully make with easily available writers from Patrick Kavanagh to Charles

Causley and Lawrence to Larkin. We have made a start on recognizing some difference between an Irish literary tradition expressed through English and a native English tradition, and recognized implicitly too that such traditions can never be wholly separated. Above all we have tried to establish a way of reading poems patiently, question by question, and of building from each poem a cumulative and augmenting sense of Heaney's work and of poetry in general. In the next chapter we can apply this method to a number of Heaney's salient areas of interest, always working through specific poems. But before going on to Chapter Two, why not read some other poems first? Look at 'Follower' (pp. 18–19) in relation to 'Digging'; 'Lovers on Aran (p. 25) and 'Shoreline' (pp. 51–2) as uses of geography to define consciousness or history and to set beside 'Bogland'; 'The Diviner' (p. 24) to amplify Heaney's sense of poetry as 'divination' in the essay 'Feeling into Words'.

2. Nature, History, Darkness

Nature into Art

In this chapter I want to look at three components of Heaney's work; the uses of nature, the impress of history, and the idea of darkness. The poems I will use to illustrate these themes will be taken from his first two books, *Death of a Naturalist* and *Door into the Dark*. *Death of a Naturalist*, Heaney's first book, was much praised for its precise observation, 'the accuracy and freshness with which sense-impressions are recorded' as Richard Kell put it, at the time of publication, in *The Guardian*.[1] And this is fair enough. Heaney's description has an exactness, a recall of its subject, which is careful and worked for. He has much the same feelings about rats as Winston Smith in George Orwell's *1984* but look at the loving attention he pays to their movements in 'An Advancement of Learning',

> . . . a rat
> Slimed out of the water . . .
> But God, another was nimbling
> Up the far bank, tracing its wet
> Arcs on the stones . . .
> He clockworked aimlessly a while,
> Stopped, back bunched and glistening,
> Ears plastered down on his knobbed skull,
> Insidiously listening.[2]

And yet Heaney's descriptions, even this early in his writing, are never straight reporting. They are made to work for the old-fashioned virtues of the English tradition and move towards some moralized conclusion which usually signals a growth in the poet's awareness. Insofar as what he describes is the natural world, it is not nature observed, but rather, nature used. And the use is for the mind. Nature is a reflex of the poet. The critic and poet, Blake Morrison, justly observes that to see Heaney as a nature poet is to thrust upon him a stereotype that doesn't really fit. Morrison prefers to see in the early books *Death of a Naturalist* and *Door into the Dark* a tendency 'to weigh inarticulacy against articulation, to acknowledge the claims of silence as well as those of speech'.[3] Heaney might be seen, within this opposition, as fighting his way out of a guarded spareness of speech, traditional to rural Northern Irish Catholics, to a pre-occupation with the eloquence of art. Another strong preoccupation often seen by critics as the focus of these early poems is 'the growth of a poet's mind', the phrase Wordsworth uses to subtitle his poem *The Prelude*. 'Digging', manifesto-like as it is, may clearly be read as about such growth. 'An Advancement of Learning' may be another, or such other poems as 'Blackberry-Picking' (p. 15), 'Churning Day' (pp. 16–17) and 'Personal Helicon' (p. 27).

Growth of a mind, observation into art, silence into speech, these all seem possible formulations and all may be helpful. This variety of understanding is suggestive about the act of criticism. Unlike some, though by no means all, of the modes of human understanding, which seek out exact definition, criticism is best seen as trying to discern relationships and order within the material it contemplates, giving it shapes that help us to hold it in our minds, rather than categories and definition that allow us to take it as read, to stop thinking about it. Morrison is right to question the foisting of a stereotype on Heaney's early work because, as the formulation hardens, so it allows us not to think, not to renew ourselves within the poems. With a view to thinking beyond the formulation, I'd like you to look at 'Death of a Naturalist' (pp. 12–13), the title poem of Heaney's first book. Read it, and then ask yourself some questions. First, think hard about the title. Is it ironic? a joke? Or is it deliberated and, like 'Digging', manifesto-like? Is the point of the poem to record a childhood fear? Or is there a wider sense of the uncontrollability, the menace, of a natural world, unamenable to and destructive of the categories of our human world? And if that should seem to be so, what if anything, might a poet do about it?

DISCUSSION

The setting and tone of the poem are not given, it should be said, in some austere and abstract high-art world but in childhood memory, again, to invoke a phrase of Wordsworth's, in a revelatory 'spot of time'.[4] The malignancy the poem will unleash is there from the beginning, 'festered in the heart', 'rotted', 'weighted down', 'sweltered', 'punishing'. But the same materials can be construed pleasurably. It is all in the point of view. It is the poet's words, not nature, which give colour. So 'bubbles gargled delicately' and there were 'dragon-flies, spotted butterflies'.

> But best of all was the warm thick slobber
> Of frogspawn that grew like clotted water
> In the shade of the banks.

Words like 'slobber' and 'clotted' are unappealing but the object they gather to – the frogspawn – is 'best of all'. Miss Walls' schoolroom lore brings homeliness to the whole thing. But then the frogs invade, 'angry', 'gross-bellied', 'cocked / On sods; their loose necks pulsed like sails'. They are full of menace and reverse the processes of nature, 'Poised like mud grenades, their blunt heads farting'. It is their vengeance on collectors of frogspawn, on the classroom domesticity of nature study, and Heaney knows that 'if' – crucial word – he dipped his hand into the flaxpond to fish it out, to put it in the jampots of poems, 'the spawn would clutch it'. It is not an invitation Heaney intends to succumb to. Neither nature nor the exact observation of the world will be central to his endeavours. Instead what he sees will chart the contours of his mind and offer itself only as analogous for what is indubitably his. The course of the poetry will be precisely to establish what is his and therefore and thereby who he is. 'Death of a Naturalist', like 'Digging', is concerned with self-definition. The difference is that where 'Digging' established Heaney as inheritor of a familial, ancestral Irish tradition, conveying his own legitimate modification of it, 'Death of a Naturalist' places him in relation to an acquired tradition.

In the poem the tradition is that of the schoolroom, perhaps especially of science and acquisitive knowledge, responding to the rawness of nature by putting it in jampots. In so far as Heaney is here defining himself within the poetic tradition he took on board at the end of 'Digging', he is moving away from the preoccupation with nature that has been a property of English writing since the Romantics and emphasizing instead that concern for self-definition which the Romantics also fostered. If this also clarifies nature, so much to the good, but it is no business of the poet to be a naturalist. And so, the poem which, at first sight, may seem a surreal and macabre account of childhood fear is, I would argue, much more a statement of Heaney's withdrawal from a concern with nature *in itself*, as something beguiling or to be investigated detachedly in its own terms. 'Death of a Naturalist' has a certain similarity to Yeats's 'Sailing to Byzantium' where the Irish poet rejects the world of nature.

> That is no country for old men. The young
> In one another's arms, birds in the trees
> – Those dying generations – at their song,
> The salmon-falls, the mackerel-crowded seas,
> Fish, flesh, or fowl, commend all summer long
> Whatever is begotten, born, and dies.[5]

It is not raw terror that Yeats feels in the face of this fecund world but a sense of its unavoidable transience, its fleeting mutability. And so he rejects it in favour of the permanence of art – 'monuments of unageing intellect'.[6] The rejection is signalled by Yeats's desire to be recast as the Byzantine golden bird.

> Once out of nature I shall never take
> My bodily form from any natural thing,
> But such a form as Grecian goldsmiths make
> Of hammered gold and gold enamelling
> To keep a drowsy Emperor awake;
> Or set upon a golden bough to sing
> To lords and ladies of Byzantium
> Of what is past, or passing, or to come.[7]

In 'Death of a Naturalist' there is no golden bird or even golden frog, but the disavowal of nature is even more graphic in that it is cast in the elaborate and luxuriant description favoured by the nature writer. Heaney can do it but he's not going to, is the idea. The basis for his refusal is a fear, at points a horror, of nature and the condition of the world, as consuming, devouring the individual and affronted by our intrusion into or comment upon it. The question is, where nature kills – 'the death of a naturalist' – can art give life? Might it only be retreat?

> I sickened, turned, and ran.

History

From the beginning of his career as poet, Heaney has based some of his most impressive poems on material drawn from history. And a sense of history – whether as archaeological evidence or in the changing fortunes of the Irish language, as shaping force or signal event – is pervasive.

It's a commonplace to see the Irish as more concerned with their history than seems reasonable – reasonable, that is, to the English. Edward Norman, in his self-styled 'external view', *A History of Modern Ireland* (1971), says, 'Irishmen are obsessed by history'.[8] The tone is mildly complaining, which seems churlish in an historian. But Irish history, if your ancestors have experienced it, is liable to engage the memory and to shape your attitudes. Ireland has been marked visibly by its history. Castles built in conquest, destroyed in combat, cottages tumbled down in evictions or decayed by the loss of their families through emigration are real, not romanticized presences in the landscape. The wasting of the country by colonial exploitation and restriction still governs the condition of Ireland, 'capitalist colonial undevelopment' as Raymond Crotty calls it in his study *Ireland in Crisis* (1986).[9] At the same time, Irish history was used by nationalists from the mid-nineteenth century on to reinforce a sense of national identity and dignity. The Irish contemplated their cultural achievements as well as they perceived their suffering. These achievements, since they were indigenous and, in the case of the literature, in the Irish not the English language, tended to define Irish society and culture, quite properly, as distinct from England's. And this, of course, had and has political implications.

Naturally, in any such construction of 'national consciousness', different components will be stressed at different times and by different people. Thus Yeats's preoccupation, in his poem 'September 1913', with the 1798 revolutionaries,

> Was it . . .
> For this Edward Fitzgerald died,
> And Robert Emmet and Wolfe Tone,
> All that delirium of the brave?[10]

is not echoed at all by Seamus Heaney. The people he records in the two poems I would like you to look at now, 'For the Commander of the *Eliza*' and 'At a Potato Digging', are to be met with in the Great Famine of the 1840s. They are not well-born and well-heeled but skeletal farm workers. The first of the poems, 'For the Commander of the *Eliza*', is in *Death of a Naturalist* (pp. 34–5). It's not included in *Selected Poems* so I will print it below. It derives from a passage in Cecil Woodham-Smith's history of the Irish Famine of 1845–49,

The Great Hunger (1962),[11] a graphically detailed and authoritative account of the Famine, which directly, by starvation and disease, indirectly by emigration, reduced Ireland's population by two million people in the 1840s.[12] Heaney prefaces his poem with a quotation from the book.

> . . . the others, with emaciated faces and prominent, staring eyeballs, were evidently in an advanced state of starvation. The officer reported to Sir James Dombrain . . . and Sir James, 'very inconveniently' wrote Routh 'interfered'.

I want to expand this quotation so that we can see more clearly the material behind Heaney's poem. With this in front of you I want you to assess the changes, omissions and additions that Heaney has made. It's both a 'spot the difference' process and also an assessment of the effect of those differences on the way we respond to the incident. The other thing I want you to consider is how effectively Heaney's poem works on its own (including his own quotation from Woodham-Smith) as a narrative. Do we really need to know more? First then, the extended quotation. The people mentioned in the passage are, in order, Charles Edward Trevelyan, who was Assistant Secretary but in effect permanent head of the Treasury; Sir Robert Peel was Prime Minister; Sir Randolph Routh was Chairman of the Relief Commission for Ireland and senior officer in the government department known as the Commissariat, which was experienced in large-scale provisioning, for example, for the British Army. Sir James Dombrain was Inspector General of the Coast Guard service and member of the Relief Commission. The time is June 1846. The question at issue here is how supplies of Indian corn, 'by no means excessive' were to be distributed during, in Routh's phrase, 'the present extraordinary dearth'. The relief committees throughout Ireland 'universally thought all their demands would be filled'. Now Woodham-Smith's full account.

> Trevelyan's intentions were very different. Irish relief was to be restricted to a single operation; the government Indian corn, purchased at the orders of Sir Robert Peel, was to be placed in the depots by the Commissariat, sold to the people – and that was the end. There was to be no replenishment, even if there was a sum of money in hand from sales; once supplies had been disposed of relief was over. In several letters, written with unusual boldness, Routh begged Trevelyan to allow further purchases. The demand on the depots was 'immense', far heavier than anything that had been anticipated, and it was increasing every day; surely the depots should remain open until September. The new potato crop would not provide any food whatsoever for the people before the middle of September at the earliest, while 'lumpers', the huge, coarse potato called the 'horse' potato, on which the people mainly depended, would not be ready until the end

of that month. Trevelyan refused; relief was to be brought to a close; possibly some depots might shut down a little later than others, but issues must shortly cease. By the end of June, 1846, government supplies were all but exhausted; on the 24th of that month, 5,000 bushels of Indian corn were all that remained in Cork and, at that, were unground, while in remote districts the people were starving. The revenue cutter, *Eliza*, making a visit of inspection, on June 22, to the Killeries, a wild district of mountain and deep ocean inlets in the far west, was implored for food by a boat-load of skeletons. The Commissariat officer at Westport, supply centre for the Killeries, had been instructed to send no more meal to the region because the depot was becoming empty.

One man, stated the officer in command, was lying on the bottom of the boat, unable to stand and already, half dead, the others, with emaciated faces and prominent, staring eyeballs, were evidently in an advanced state of starvation. The officer reported to Sir James Dombrain, Inspector-General of the Coastguard Service, who had served on relief during the famine of 1839, and Sir James Dombrain, 'very inconveniently', wrote Routh, 'interfered'. He 'prevailed' on an officer at the Westport depot to issue meal, which he gave away free; he also 'prevailed' on the captain of the Government steamship, *Rhadamanthus*, to take 100 tons of meal, intended for Westport, to the Coastguard station at the Killeries, 'The Coast Guard with all their zeal and activity are too lavish', wrote Routh to Trevelyan.[13]

Now here is 'For the Commander of the *Eliza*'. Make a note of the principal way in which it differs from the prose account.

Routine patrol off West Mayo; sighting
A rowboat heading unusually far
Beyond the creek, I tacked and hailed the crew
In Gaelic. Their stroke had clearly weakened
As they pulled to, from guilt or bashfulness
I was conjecturing when, O my sweet Christ,
We saw piled in the bottom of their craft
Six grown men with gaping mouths and eyes
Bursting the sockets like spring onions in drills.
Six wrecks of bone and pallid, tautened skin.
'Bia, bia,
Bia'. In whines and snarls their desperation
Rose and fell like a flock of starving gulls.
We'd known about the shortage but on board
They always kept us right with flour and beef
So understand my feelings, and the men's,
Who had no mandate to relieve distress
Since relief was then available in Westport –
Though clearly these poor brutes would never make it.
I had to refuse food: they cursed and howled
Like dogs that had been kicked hard in the privates.
When they drove at me with their starboard oar
(Risking capsize themselves) I saw they were

Violent and without hope. I hoisted
And cleared off. Less incidents the better.

Next day, like six bad smells, those living skulls
Drifted through the dark of bunks and hatches
And once in port I exorcised my ship
Reporting all to the Inspector General.
Sir James, I understand, urged free relief
For famine victims in the Westport Sector
And earned tart reprimand from good Whitehall.
Let natives prosper by their own exertions;
Who could not swim might go ahead and sink.
'The Coast Guard with their zeal and activity
Are too lavish' were the words, I think.

DISCUSSION

The poem celebrates a frustrated act of humanity on the part of an English naval captain and Sir James Dombrain, Inspector-General of the Coastguard Service. Given the material that Heaney had available there are other ways the poem might have been written. An 'external' view might have wished to portray Dombrain and the captain as meddlers in the higher reaches of Whitehall policy. Why was Trevelyan interested in limiting the supply of Indian meal? Given limited stocks might it not be right to keep up the Westport depot? And so on. There are other ways of looking at things. 'Let natives prosper by their own exertions' is Heaney's clue to Trevelyan's approach. But Heaney is not primarily concerned with the mysteries of government administration but about the rigours of famine and the act of compassion of the two men actually on the scene. In particular the poem is a tribute more than a hundred years later to an unknown sea-captain. Notice, incidentally, one of the hazards of this sort of comparison with sources, which is so common in academic criticism. How do I know that Heaney is not using a much fuller source than Woodham-Smith for his information, say the captain's report? I don't. It's only probability that he isn't. So I can't make any very precise claims about what Heaney is trying to do. That would be altogether too circumstantial. Keep this in mind as you read what follows, in so far as it presents an account of Heaney's methods and intentions.

First, it does seem to me that the poem, with the aid of Heaney's brief quotation from *The Great Hunger*, is perfectly explicable. That is to say that, in terms of the poem's effect and clarity, we don't really need the additional information that the longer quotation from Woodham-Smith provides. It may be of use in clarifying the nature of the famine and some of the complexities of relief administration and so it does undoubtedly add to our sum of knowledge. But the poem works well without any of that. We do not need to know who in particular Routh is, only that in the poem he represents, or stands for, Whitehall. Any estimate of Routh's overall stance in discussions – for example, that 'in several letters, written with unusual boldness, Routh begged Trevelyan to allow further purchases' – is not relevant to the poem. Nor do we need to know the extent to which Sir James Dombrain tried to help, in diverting a hundred tons of meal on board *The Rhadamanthus*. Instead Heaney contrasts human feeling on the spot, 'O my sweet Christ', with remote administration, 'good Whitehall', where the irony of 'good' adds to our sense of the captain's humanity. And he examines too the problem of the chain of command, 'no mandate to relieve distress', 'I had to refuse food', the whole range of moral questions that obeying orders can confuse. At the same time Heaney develops both the captain's character and the placing of the incident by quick, economic strokes in the narrative, 'routine patrol off West Mayo', 'less incidents the better'. And one touch that is not hinted in Woodham-Smith's account, 'I tacked and hailed the crew / In Gaelic'. The rowboat's crew are Irish speakers, 'Bia, bia, / Bia' (food, food, food) and, by that fact, part of a different culture and people. The captain recognizes that difference and is attuned to it. Another difference of emphasis is in Heaney's line 'since relief was then available in Westport' where Woodham-Smith says 'the depot was becoming empty'. The two statements are not incompatible. Both are explanations for there being no relief available outside Westport. Heaney's line places emphasis on its selective but actual availability while Woodham-Smith emphasizes the danger that even the Westport depot might run out unless stocks were conserved. What justifies Heaney's emphasis is that Sir James Dombrain, on the spot, did feel that diverting the meal to the Killeries, the scene of the *Eliza's* meeting with the rowboat, was both necessary and possible. One other thing Heaney does. A cutter is essentially a small manoeuvrable patrol boat and nothing in the situation of the poem suggests otherwise. But taking advantage of the name *Eliza* with its Tudor ring Heaney gives the incident an imperial echo. In the title 'For the Commander of the *Eliza*', it sounds more like a ship of the line. And giving the captain the title 'Commander' does the same thing.

The great difference though between the two descriptions is in the way Heaney has filled out, made eloquent the incident, so that rather than being, as in Woodham-Smith's detailed narrative, one more fact in an accumulation of facts, it becomes a story which indicts an inhuman policy and at the same time celebrates human kindness. He takes a fact and bestows a gift, a libation to an otherwise unknown officer. Heaney's art usually tends towards 'lyric', a mode which shapes and formalizes experience from the particular to the general. But there is also, not far beneath the surface, a strong vein of narrative interest. Much Irish twentieth-century literary distinction has been located in the short story and in particular with Frank O'Connor, Liam O'Flaherty and Sean O'Faolain.[14] Heaney seizes upon and builds the significant moment much as they do.

I've raised the question of the usefulness or not of consulting source materials when trying to read a poem and I've been at least cautious about the use of sources. Some readers seem to be positively helped by the sort of detail that poets often feel to be extraneous. Poets mostly, if not invariably, feel that their poems stand sufficiently explained in the words which they have chosen to put down on the page and by any notes they have themselves supplied. I am speaking here of sources and not of the wider attuning to a poet's work which is often, a bit regrettably, called 'background'. I say regrettably because 'background' suggests that the whole world is somehow existing to project this particular poem up front, which few poets, I think, would ever claim. Poems are more like the pulse by which we sense the blood flow and the body's welfare than the body and blood itself. By that function, of course, they are indivisible from it, from the blood and body of the world.

But some readers are undoubtedly helped by sources, in the sense that they know that line 3 might be a quotation from Maeterlinck which the poet read one day while sitting in his garden, say, in Wantage. The poet hasn't told us this but academic ferretting has, with modest triumph, established it.

'Background' is a much more important matter. One of the difficulties of writing poetry these days, it's often alleged, is that you can't rely on a common stock of knowledge in your assumed readership. Milton, the suggestion is, could assume such a readership who would know their Bible and their Classics; so could Pope. When this common audience disappeared is anybody's guess; perhaps with the advent of Universal Education. The argument, whichever way it goes, is crude. Any poet who can at setting out assume a readership is probably already out of date. A poet creates and leads a readership. And I doubt that is any harder or easier than it ever was. Audiences simply change. Milton's seventeenth-century readership or Pope's eighteenth-century readership do not at all coincide socially with the type of readership that Hughes or Heaney might today attract. The audiences have different tastes, knowledge and expectations. It is not unreasonable that Heaney or Derek Walcott should hope that an audience in England might acquaint themselves a little with at least an outline of Irish or West Indian history, either from wanting to be in touch, or from sympathy or because they have liked their poems and want to extend the knowledge they can themselves bring to their reading. The knowledge is a good in itself. The fact that some have it before they first read the poem and others catch up on it, that is, that some of the audience is assumed and some acquired, is neither here nor there.

I'd like you now to read perhaps the finest of Heaney's early poems, 'At a Potato Digging' (pp. 21–3). Are there ways in which you could relate the poem to the first poem we looked at, 'Digging'? And differences to be noted? Look very closely at the words and images Heaney uses. Do you detect any recurring associations which might give clues to Heaney's attitude to the actions he describes? Do you notice anything different about the way Heaney uses history here as compared with 'For the Commander of the *Eliza*'?

DISCUSSION

'At a Potato Digging' projects the past into the present, and finds no discontinuity between the two. While retaining the image of digging the potatoes,

> . . . that we picked
> Loving their cool hardness in our hands.
>
> ('Digging', p. 10)

Heaney widens its implications from a sense of his family and its ancestry to the ancestry of all Ireland, the terrible and total history that the land enshrines.

Yet the poem does not begin with history. If anything its opening image, 'A mechanical digger wrecks the drill', suggests a poem about the present, though rejecting it, in the sense that modern farming techniques destroy some ancestral relationship between man and land. But the digger is no more than an aid and it cannot destroy, only re-express that relationship. The relationship however is not to be romanticized. To refer again to Patrick Kavanagh, and in particular Heaney's essay on him 'From Monaghan to the Grand Canal' in *Preoccupations*, Heaney there argues that Kavanagh's poem *The Great Hunger*

> consciously rejects the Yeatsian 'dream of the noble and the beggar-man'. It is a rebuke to the idea of the peasant as noble savage and a dramatization of what its author called 'the usual barbaric life of the Irish country poor'. Against the paternalistic magnificence of
>
> John Synge, I, and Augusta Gregory thought
> All that we did, all that we said or sang

> Must come from contact with the soil, from that
> Contact everything, Antaeus-like, grew strong

– against this we must set Section XII of the Kavanagh poem which answers it with a vision of 'the peasant ploughman who is half a vegetable', 'a sick horse nosing around the meadow for a clean place to die'.[15]

Similarly, in 'At a Potato Digging' all the movements and images of Section I are stern and unrelenting in their sense of unremitting labour, 'swarm', 'stoop to fill', 'fingers go dead', 'like crows attacking crow-black fields', 'straighten', 'stand tall', and 'stumble', 'bow', 'bend' and 'fumble'. Such labour, runs the implication, has been unremitting through centuries. The 'higgledy line', the 'ragged ranks' have the disordered bearing of many past Irish collective movements, whether following a charismatic leader or a corpse to burial. The rhythm of the work is as inevitable in its retreat and return as the sea, which is constantly suggested in the images, 'dark shower', 'wicker creels', 'from hedge to headland', 'keep breaking', 'fish a new load from the crumbled surf'. But the subject is the land, treated as deity, 'the black Mother' and the actions of work are seen as, at the same time, acts of propitiation, 'Heads bow, trunks bend', in 'processional stooping', through 'centuries' of 'homage to the famine god'. Potato digging 'recurs mindlessly as autumn', the 'altar of the sod' is 'seasonal' and so the presence of the mechanical digger is continuous, even identical with all the diggings of the past. Present time becomes liturgical time by whose means history is stabilized and repeated in the present. This section has been tightly rhymed in a basically 10-syllable line. In the succeeding stanzas the rhymes are less regular and less formed and the lines are shorter, 8- or, in Section III, 7-syllables. This quickens the beat. It is as if Section I implicitly contains all that has to be said, and the succeeding sections are comments making the thought explicit. Accordingly Section II describes the object of the 'cultus', the potato. The terms used, even as the potato's goodness is celebrated, carry a macabre edge. Its colours are stark, 'flint-white, purple'. If there is intended here a continuation of the liturgical image, then white is the colour of joy and purple, of penance, so the potato symbolizes the range of human response. The imagery is slightly distorted or grotesque, 'inflated', 'native to the black hutch', 'halved seed shot and clotted', 'knobbed', 'slit-eyed', 'petrified hearts'. (The Irish custom is, incidentally, to cut the seed potatoes in half, an eye to a half, to make them go further – hence 'halved seed'.) On this ambiguous basis, however, the potatoes nonetheless turn out to be good.

> . . . Split
> by the spade, they show white as cream.

There are 'good smells', 'a clean birth', 'solid feel'. The potatoes are piled in pits for storage and again the macabre imagery returns. They are 'live skulls, blind-eyed'. This description immediately opens Section III, a description not of potatoes but of people, skeletal, searching the land for food in the 1845 Famine and eating potatoes poisoned by the blight. 'Higgledy' used in Section I to describe the labourers of the present day, and used again here, connects the mid-nineteenth century living skeletons with today's potato gatherers. Unlike Christ, this god does not live again after having 'lain three days in the long clay pit'. It does not restore people to life. Instead 'Millions rotted along with it', and the macabre images of Section II are fully realized in 'a people hungering from birth', and the smell, still perceptible, of 'the running sore'. The images of Section III are like medieval emblems.

> Live skulls, blind-eyed, balanced on
> wild higgledy skeletons

suggests a dance of death, and there are allegorical expressions, 'beaks of famine snipped at guts', 'Hope rotted like a marrow'. Section IV pulls the poem back from these savageries. In tight rhyming stanzas, echoing but lightening the line of Section I by shortening it, the rhythm of the dance and the work 'deadens, the workers stop'. The birds, the attacking crows, of Section I, 'the plucked birds' and 'beaks of famine' of Section III, become 'a gay flotilla of gulls'. The workers 'flop down in the ditch' but it is in restoring rest, not in death. They eat and drink 'tea in bright canfuls' and break in thanksgiving 'timeless fasts'. The ground, ambiguous to the last, is still 'faithless' but on it, as in an ancient religion, they 'spill libations' and 'scatter crusts', gifts to 'the black Mother' of Section I, 'The bitch earth' of Section III. In 'Digging' Heaney decides to dig with the pen. In 'Death of a Naturalist', faced with natural horror, he sickens, turns and runs. In 'At a Potato Digging' the ancestral continuity which had been claimed in 'Digging' is amplified and widened from the family alone to the sense of a nation, one in history and experience. The horror is outfaced and assuaged in an act of devotion, libations spilt on the ground. Where 'For the Commander of the *Eliza*' is specific to its compassionate moment in June 1846, inviting us to infer its wider circumstances in statecraft and politics, 'At a Potato Digging' embraces the past in the present. It is not to be read as sociological comment on the power and circumstance of famine but as an act of love. Again we can invoke Heaney on Kavanagh

> if *The Great Hunger* [Kavanagh's poem] did not exist, a greater hunger would, the hunger of a culture for its own image and expression.

> It is a poem of its own place and time, transposing the griefs of the past – its title conventionally refers to the Great Famine of the 1840s – into the distress of the present, as significant in the Irish context as Hardy's novels were in the English, socially committed but also committed to a larger, more numinous concept of love whose function he decreed was not to look back but 'to look on'.[16]

It is in such a transposition and such a cultural expression that we can most fruitfully locate Heaney's use of history. In this connection you could read 'Requiem for the Croppies' (p. 33), a poem about the Irish Rebellion of 1798. In *Preoccupations* (p. 56) Heaney tells us that he wrote the poem in 1966, the fiftieth anniversary of the 1916 Rising in Ireland. The poem incorporates 'an image of resurrection' which links the 1798 'croppies' and the events of Easter 1916. He concludes, 'I did not realize at the time that the original heraldic murderous encounter between Protestant yeoman and Catholic rebel was to be initiated again in the summer of 1969, in Belfast, two months after the book [*Door into the Dark*] was published'. Do you feel that sometimes political or social circumstances will alter the meanings we take from poems?

Darkness

The imagery of darkness is especially potent in Heaney's poetry, and most of all in his second book, *Door into the Dark* (1969). This title comes from the first line of 'The Forge' (*Selected Poems*, p. 30)

> All I know is a door into the dark.

I want, with a few side-trips, to concentrate on 'The Forge'. What I hope will happen here is that we will seek out the meanings and implications in the language of the poems, in a pretty intensive way. There's always a danger in this that we might overread, 'seeing more in Homer, than Homer knew', or at least, than Heaney intends. But Heaney is a deliberate writer and overreading means we do at least read, whereas underreading means we don't quite read. The elements in the poem I want you to concentrate on are the blacksmith, the anvil and 'the dark' itself. What meanings can you assign to them? Are there odd elements in the description of blacksmith and anvil – not perhaps discordant ones, but certainly drawn from different ranges of expression? A way of assessing this, perhaps, is to ask, would the blacksmith say that about himself or the anvil? Or is Heaney talking for him or about him? We can use our knowledge from other Heaney poems to help us here. For the figure of the blacksmith and his craft, you could recall 'Digging' – you'll know it by heart now – and for the image of darkness, does 'Bogland' present any similar pattern or movement? What I am hoping for is something similar to what happened with the drawing out of the waves of images in 'At a Potato Digging'. Ultimately I want our attention to be concentrated on this fruitful image of 'the dark' and to fit it into the wide tradition that I think is implied. But we must attend first to its context here and now – the way it appears in this particular poem, which you should now read.

DISCUSSION

Heaney begins

> All I know is a door into the dark.

Outside, and prelude to the darkness, is a mess of bits and pieces, 'old axles and iron hoops rusting', inside the sound of hammer on anvil, and 'the unpredictable fantail of sparks', or the hiss of a new shoe as it toughens in water. Heaney, in the darkness, surmises some central place of activity

> The anvil must be somewhere in the centre, . . .
> Set there immoveable: an altar
> Where he expends himself in shape and music.

Occasionally the blacksmith breaks off from work to lean on the door jamb and remember the days when there were lots of horses where now, in the street, there are cars. And then he goes in,

> . . . with a slam and a flick
> To beat real iron out, to work the bellows.

So what have we here? First, perhaps, we should notice that Heaney is making the blacksmith a figure of the artist and so of himself. The trick of this is to do it so that you don't destroy the man's credibility as a blacksmith and make him a mere symbol. Does Heaney make the blacksmith perfectly credible? I think so. Little touches help, touches that we cannot force into the necessities of symbol but are part of the blacksmith's own mind or appearance, 'hairs in his nose', and the way he 'recalls a clatter of hoofs where traffic is flashing in rows'. This is a different sort of statement from the description of the anvil as 'an altar / Where he expends himself in shape and music'. But each plays its part in the poem, the first to preserve the real and living situation, the other to give that life an extension, a further life in wider ranges of meaning. Heaney wants to keep hold of both aspects – and, indeed, doesn't, I think, really see them as divisible. It's a question of what, at each point, he wishes to stress. At this point the title, 'The Forge', takes on additional significance. It was James Joyce's idea of Stephen Dedalus's vocation as an artist that he would 'forge in the smithy of my soul the uncreated conscience of my race'[17]

– the Irish race. It is not a presumption that Heaney seems to share. The race is there, *and* its conscience. He only seeks to add to its achievements, to expend 'himself in shape and music', and to be a party to the 'unpredictable fantail of sparks'. That seems to be enough to be going on with, without taking on the burdens of the race. Heaney's metaphors are indicative pictures, shaped morals, 'to beat real iron out, to work the bellows' where the words 'real' and 'work' carry an implicit assertion about the validity of Heaney's own work. Heaney, as artist, really digs just as his father did. The blacksmith as artist beats 'real' iron. And Heaney is digger–blacksmith–artist. In some sense such preoccupation is a seeking after assurance, but at the same time it asserts the grounds for such assurance. We should be attentive to the anvil too. Heaney says it 'must be somewhere in the centre' that is, at the heart of things, the point of control. It is described as a strange and composite object, 'horned as a unicorn', a creature, elegant, mysterious, and legendary but real enough in the imagination, and then, 'at one end square'. 'Square' is the abstract expression of solidity and order, the property that more than anything gives the strength that makes the anvil 'immoveable'. The anvil is 'an altar', composed, therefore, of honest graft and imagination and the blacksmith serves it like a priest, his vestment, a leather apron, his liturgy 'shape and music'.

But Heaney draws attention, in the title of the book in which this poem appears, to the phrase 'a door into the dark', and, in an apparently extravagant assertion, he says it is 'all I know'. The extravagance is in the negativity. Mostly when we say 'I know' we are representing our control over some area of knowledge, even of insight. Thus 'I know that my Redeemer liveth' or from 'The Ode on a Grecian Urn',

> Beauty is truth, truth beauty, – that is all
> Ye know on earth and all ye need to know.[18]

where Keats, or rather the Grecian Urn, desperately tries to assert a knowledge which the substance of the poem, with its unfulfilled lovers, deserted town, heifer intended for sacrifice, uncompleted sacrifice and in general, cold pastoral, seems to belie. Heaney echoing the same word 'all' seems rather less bold. 'All I know' he says 'is a door into the dark'. This is not the assertion, apparently, of an extensive knowledge. It might seem desperate, even. And yet, isn't it rather self-effacing? Heaney clearly knows and relishes a great many things. The poems we have read indicate a very aware, intelligent and informed poet. Can 'a door into the dark' render that? Well, of course, once inside the dark, we do meet quite substantial presences, work, an anvil–altar, a blacksmith–artist, shape and music, real iron-poems. There is nothing desperate about it. Perhaps 'a door into the dark' is a real way in. After all, what is outside? – 'old axles and iron hoops rusting'. But there is more going on in the phrase than a simple reversal of our expectation of the word 'dark'. Expectations depend very much on what we already know and 'dark' for Heaney is not, and has not been, a negative condition. It is also not a word for which we could simply substitute 'interior' and see it only as a figure of self-exploration in psychological terms.

'Darkness' has further reaches which go well beyond self-exploration. It is solidly established in the language of spirituality where it figures as a possible, even necessary condition for our knowing at all. The word resonates in mystical theology and is given much of its excitement for a poet by the sixteenth-century Spanish theologian and poet St John of the Cross whose work is to appear later in Heaney's 'Station Island'. St John of the Cross, commenting on the phrase 'en la noche serena' (in the serene night) from stanza 38 of his *Spiritual Canticle*, sees 'contemplation' as 'dark' and argues that God teaches the soul 'as in the silence and quiet of the night, hidden by darkness from all that is of the senses and of nature'.[19]

This is the intellectual tradition within which we should understand Heaney's use of dark or 'negative' images. Roughly speaking, in mystical theology, there are two modes by which knowledge of God may occur, the 'positive way' and the 'negative way'. In the 'positive way' understanding of God proceeds through an understanding of His creation, by analogy. It is fairly clear that poets, supposing they wish to approach God, will habitually be rather more likely to go about it this way, by contemplating indicative objects. And, of course, all objects are indicative if you can only see them right. 'Outside, old axles and iron hoops rusting' will do as well as anything else.

This is, in part, to be understood as a kind of shorthand for entry into the variety of creation. It is the positive way at its most apparent. The traditional modes of meditation will clearly work simply as techniques of understanding, as modes of entry into the way things are. In the 'negative way' the opposite strategy is at work, but the end paradoxically is the same, an entry into understanding. God is seen as essentially so different from His creation that comparison is logically excluded as a means of knowledge. We can only see Him as not like anything we can perceive and register on the senses. This is the force behind, for example, the Victorian hymn

Immortal, invisible God only wise
In light inaccessible hid from our eyes

which derives from a text like *Isaiah*, xlv.15:

> Verily Thou art a God that hidest Thyself.

T. S. Eliot seems to describe an entry into knowledge while the senses are suspended in *The Waste Land*

> I could not
> Speak, and my eyes failed, I was neither
> Living nor dead, and I knew nothing,
> Looking into the heart of light, the silence.[20]

Since God is utterly unlike, we exclude the senses and the world, as means towards understanding. In so far as we wish to describe this procedure, negative descriptions are used not because they are in any way close but because they indicate most clearly the inadequacy of our means of approach and so the splendour of what we approach. In consequence the 'dark' represents a splendour, something to be sought. It means the same as, in the positive way, the 'light' does. Nonetheless the exclusion and frustration of the senses is painful to us and so the path towards God, in this tradition, must pass through pain. The pain is at the same time given dignity by the end, the understanding, which it precedes. Again these procedures may operate, as a matter of temperament, as a means towards any type of understanding, religious or not. It might be said that the negative way implies understanding a thing in its own terms. Shakespeare's sonnet 130 'My mistress' eyes are nothing like the sun' works like this. Such a method might lead to a non-metaphorical poetry if pursued single-mindedly. But what needs to be stressed here is that these modes, the 'positive' and the 'negative' are not, for the poet, mutually exclusive. Habituated to metaphor and operating in knowledge of the tradition, as Heaney is, 'the dark' becomes a metaphor for 'the infinite' or 'knowledge' or 'understanding', for whatever is seen to be the goal. It becomes an image alongside other images. We have looked at 'Bogland', the final poem in *Door into the Dark*, and seen how the related metaphor of the bottomless boghole expresses infinity. In turn it epitomizes the whole landscape of Ireland, and this is understood as a 'positive view', an infinite depth, with past culture layered on past culture, all perceived in a present which, like the bog, is continuous with them all.

Another relevant poem is 'In Gallarus Oratory', which is in *Door into the Dark* (p. 22) though not in *Selected Poems*. In it Heaney shows how the image of darkness can itself become a container for more clearly positive images.

> You can still feel the community pack
> This place: it's like going into a turfstack,

A core of old dark walled up with stone
A yard thick. When you're in it alone
You might have dropped, a reduced creature
To the heart of the globe. No worshipper
Would leap up to his God off this floor.

Founded there like heroes in a barrow
They sought themselves in the eye of their King
Under the black weight of their own breathing.
And how he smiled on them as out they came,
The sea a censer, and the grass a flame.

Gallarus is an early Christian boat-shaped oratory on the Dingle Peninsula, in County Kerry. In a talk on Early Irish Nature Poetry, in 1978, reprinted in *Preoccupations*, Heaney says

> Inside, in the dark of the stone, it feels as if you are sustaining a great pressure, bowing under like the generations of monks who must have bowed down in meditation and reparation on that floor. I felt the weight of Christianity, in all its rebuking aspects, its calls to self-denial and self-abnegation, its humbling of the proud flesh and insolent spirit. But coming out of the cold heart of the stone, into the sunlight

Interior of Gallarus Oratory, 'A core of old dark walled up with stone . . .'.

> and the dazzle of grass and sea, I felt a lift in my heart, a surge towards happiness that must have been experienced over and over again by those monks as they crossed that same threshold centuries ago.[21]

and he speaks of 'this surge towards praise, this sudden apprehension of the world as light, as illumination'. Now you could see these two worlds of darkness and pressure and of light and dazzle as opposed. And oppose Christianity with Nature, self-denial with the self at the same time, and for good measure. It's often enough done and the terms invite us to. But you can also see them as complementary, and so Heaney seems to see them, here indeed and perhaps even more clearly in the poem he wrote closer to the visit. Inside it is, as Heaney exactly puts it, 'a core of old dark walled up with stone'. The pressure upon you is downwards. As he describes it

> No worshipper
> Would leap up to his God off this floor.

But from the state of a 'reduced creature', 'heroes in a barrow', as it were entombed, inside, seeking themselves

> in the eye of their King
> Under the black weight of their own breathing

the community expands and dilates as they return to a world made into a wider image of their worship

> And how he smiled on them as out they came,
> The sea a censer, and the grass a flame.

This is a triumphant re-entry into a transfigured world of perceptions, rhetorical as a trumpet-call, but actually dependent on the initial withdrawal from the senses into the 'core of old dark'. It is fair to say then that the image of dark is an image among images for Heaney, but it is an important one, not just because he bothers to call one of his books *Door into the Dark* but because it is procedural and temperamental. His relish at creation is obvious, easy to pick up. Nobody describes objects as well as he does without relishing them. Also it's what poets are supposed to do. But equally, Heaney sees them as illuminated by withdrawal from them. The truth about them may not be revealed simply by involvement in them. When later in his work political questions about the North of Ireland become dominant, this distinction will be helpful as a structuring device in locating his position.

Meanwhile you could look at 'The Barn' (p. 14), a more naturalistic, less analogical treatment of the image of darkness. And notice in this poem an accompanying childhood terror. 'Personal Helicon' (p. 27) would pay rereading too. And look at 'The Peninsula' (p. 32), a poem where a stark and almost minimal sense of the landscape is seen as the necessary structure for experience, a means to 'uncode all landscapes'. This reduction has some kinship with the ideas I have tried to develop through the image of darkness.

In this Chapter I've looked at three themes in Heaney's writing; nature, history and darkness understood as revelation. To extend these ideas and to involve other traditions in them you could look at three of Heaney's essays in *Preoccupations*, 'Englands of the Mind' (pp. 150–69) – about other histories; 'In the Country of Convention: English Pastoral Verse' (pp. 173–80), with its attention to other uses of nature; and 'The God in the Tree: Early Irish Nature Poetry' (pp. 181–9) from which I quoted Heaney's description of Gallarus Oratory.

3. Image, Language, Distance

In this chapter I'm going to ask you to read groups of poems, rather than just one or two, and to concentrate on each group from a particular angle. I'll focus each section on some aspect of Heaney's use of language and invite you to read several poems to illustrate and amplify his usage. The first section is to do with a particular sort of image he uses in many of the poems in *Door into the Dark*. I am calling it the self-reflexive image.

Self-reflexive imagery

An image is a mechanism by which we describe or explain one thing in terms of or by comparison with another. Normally the elements of the comparison are known to be distinct even though there is something similar about them. It's the point of similarity, of course, which allows us to compare them. An example would be the description of the seed in 'The Wife's Tale', (pp. 35–6) 'It was hard as shot, / Innumerable and cool'. Shot is known to be distinct from seed, but its hardness, quantity and coolness invite comparison without blurring the distinction. A slightly more complex example is in

'Shoreline' (pp. 51–2) where the sea is described as 'a grey bottom with puddles / Dead-eyed as fish', and where the sea, the puddles and the dead eyes of the fish are netted together by the syntactical doubt as to whether it's the sea or the puddles or both that are 'dead-eyed as fish'. The prevailing grey tone and suggestion of similar shapes (puddles, eyes), also bring the elements of the description very tight into each other, but we still know that the fish, the eyes, the sea and the puddles are different. In the self-reflexive image the terms of the image are self-referring. To be absolutely clear as to the structure of these images, here is an example which isn't in the *Selected Poems*. In 'Girls Bathing, Galway 1965' (from *Door into the Dark*)

> The breakers pour
> Themselves into themselves, the years
> Shuttle through space invisibly.[1]

where the breakers pour nothing other than themselves into nothing other than themselves. The movement between their parts (the breakers) is therefore self-coalescing. A number of critics, including Christopher Ricks and Neil Corcoran, have drawn attention to imagery of this type and not only in Heaney's work.[2] The elements have been described as self-involved or self-inwoven, reflexive. I have chosen to give the screw one extra turn and call it, at the risk of tautology, self-reflexive. This is to suggest two things, the extreme degree of interwovenness in the terms of the image and the degree to which the poet's own mental procedures, his 'self', might be deduced from the use of such images.

Let me first look at some more examples of such images. Most of 'At Ardboe Point' (pp. 38–9), is given over to a description of a cloud of mosquitoes, thick and drifting, by the lough shore. The insects are described as having individual and separable existence, 'a pumping body', but are mostly presented by Heaney collectively 'a smoke of flies', 'a hail of fine chaff'. So far this is straightforward metaphor but, in the stanza describing how they form a shifting singular body as the car drives through them, the image takes on a more reflexive quality.

> Yet we leave no clear wake
> For they open and close on us
> As the air opens and closes.
> (p. 38)

This sense of a singular body as indistinguishable as air is achieved, in part at least, by the repetition of the two verbs 'open' and 'close', in the description first of the insects and then of the air. It is a coalescing device, as if we are not describing separable things, 'insects' and 'air', but a singular existence which is both 'insects' and 'air' and indistinguishable into its components. In the final two stanzas the insects' lives become their heaven, through which they die.

> For these are our innocent, shuttling
> Choirs, dying through
> Their own live empyrean.
>
> (p. 39)

It is innocence to create, to live and to die one's own heaven, 'their own live empyrean'. The whole poem is built from a coalescing sense of the world's presence, insects, air, heaven, life and death. It is not merely that a network is built between individual items but that the items become identities. Incidentally, the use of the word 'our' claims them as Irish insects. Heaney resists the term 'mosquitoes' as conjuring up 'forests' and 'swamps', altogether alien, not 'our' own innocent creatures. In that sense they become homely, secure through familiarity, not 'troublesome'. You will find other examples of this self-inwound imagery if you read 'The Given Note' (p. 48) where 'this air' – eventually a melody – comes to the fiddler 'out of the night', 'coming in on loud weather', possibly to be called 'spirit music', 'out of wind' coming from 'mid-Atlantic' or 'nowhere'. At the end of the poem

> It comes off the bow gravely,
> Rephrases itself into the air.
>
> (p. 48)

This is another coalescing, facilitated by the different meanings, the pun implied in 'air'. Of course a pun, different meanings in the one word, is the fullest degree of reflexivity, of self-referral. Although I'm concerned to isolate this as one of Heaney's techniques, we still must assess the particular meanings of each usage. In this poem, is some kind of analogy being presented for the processes of art, its derivation from and its return to the world?

My last illustration is the poem 'Undine' (p. 34). An undine is a female elemental spirit of the water and, as we can see in 'Girls Bathing, Galway 1965', water is an excellent medium for this coalescing imagery. Water assumes the form into which it flows, and this enables Heaney to describe clearing ditches in this poem in extraordinary ways which may seem fanciful, certainly not as hard-headed as 'Digging' was.

> . . . he dug a spade deep in my flank
> And took me to him. I swallowed his trench
>
> Gratefully, dispersing myself for love
> Down in his roots, climbing his brassy grain –

and finally

He explored me so completely, each limb
Lost its cold freedom. Human, warmed to him.
(p. 34)

There is a huge degree of reflexivity in 'Undine'. Is Heaney using the image of clearing ditches, permitting water to flow through them and so through the whole of agriculture, 'roots', 'grain' and therefore, through culture itself, as an image of sexual union? Or is he using the language of sexual union to present precisely that mythic account of the development of culture, through the human taming of the elements? This would restore a lot of the original meaning of an undine as a supernatural spirit, inhabiting, even personifying, the water. Or is Heaney doing a third thing, presenting a texture so inwound, so much referring to the elements that compose it, that he provides a structure that does not refer simply to sexuality or cultural history, but incorporates both into an image of unity itself? The poem would be seen as an analogue, a symbolic equivalence for a wished-for, even a perceived state, so harmonious that we cannot distinguish its parts. I present this series of questions not to provoke answers. As to answers, your rational guess is as good as mine. But, as to poems, it is their particular quality to allow all the questions and all the answers to remain present and to constitute the mysteriousness of the world we seek to comment on. They do not codify the world so much as invite it into perception.

I would like you now to read 'The Plantation' (pp. 49–50) and then 'A Lough Neagh Sequence' (pp. 40–7), Heaney's most sustained use of this self-reflexive imagery. Are we entitled to see this sort of image, not just as poetic technique, but as a recurring mental structure in Heaney's approach to things? If it is such a characteristic pattern of thought, can we assign a meaning not just to the images or poems individually but to the recurring structures of thought itself? Is a concern with self-reflexive imagery to be considered as, say, a concern with unity, or with bringing things into unity?

A little note on Lough Neagh. It's a large inland stretch of water west of Belfast and with its eighty miles of shore in Derry, Antrim, Armagh, Down and Tyrone. It is drained by the River Bann at Toomebridge. Its waters are said to have petrifying qualities, 'virtue that hardens wood to stone' as Heaney says. There is an old rhyme

Lough Neagh hones! Lough Neagh hones!
You put 'em in sticks and you take 'em out stones.

I've raised some large issues just now, inviting you to draw parallels between a number of poems, one a longish sequence. But as always first read the poems for themselves. In 'A Lough Neagh Sequence' keep an eye on the eels and the wakes of the boats. And with 'The

Plantation', do you find the landscape in the poem reassuring or disturbing?

DISCUSSION

In *Door into the Dark*, Heaney regularly works with images that blur into one another or are self-reflexive. We could go further and describe the effect of this. It helps produce a riddling tone, precisely because the elements of the poem are so tightly bound into one another. 'Undine', for example, is a spectacular intermingling of man, water, spirit and woman. In 'The Given Note' (p. 48), air, art, wind and spirit are not distinct. 'The Plantation', however, far from benignly coalescing spirit and elements, presents a nightmarish landscape, confusing by its repetitiousness. The wood has a fairytale atmosphere and yet is humanly sullied. To the 'all comers', attracted in from the road that hedges it, its limits seem defined 'from outside' but, in reality, it resists definition as much as any space in a Kafka story or a Pinter play. The final coalescing, in which 'you', venturing into the woods, become all the characters, pilot, stray, Hansel, Gretel and witch, is not reassuring or resolved. The possibilities are not so much mysterious and resonant as problematic and disturbing.

In 'A Lough Neagh Sequence', the opening poem 'Up the Shore' (p. 40) sets the scene, the geographical location, the peculiar quality of the lough's waters, but also a sense of historical continuity, 'The lough will claim a victim every year'. In the face of this, the fishermen collaborate with fate 'and never learn to swim'. But there is another collusion, with the eels. Instead of lifting five hundred stone in one go, as the men do at Toomebridge weirs, 'up the shore' in Antrim and Tyrone 'they confront them one by one'. It is the eel's sinuosity, its movement through land and water between Lough Neagh and the Sargasso Sea, which provides the compacting image of the sequence. The eels are creatures well in keeping with the coalescing images that feature in *Door into the Dark* and the poems rejoice in describing them, 'hungering down each undulation', knitted 'four-ply' and 'sucked home like lubrication'. In the final poem of the sequence, 'Vision' (p. 47), the sense of horror comes to fullness as the eels move 'like hatched fears' through the grass and the observer relives childhood fantasies of being dragged to the water by a rope of lice. Time, Heaney says, confirms 'the horrid cable'. Equally the fishermen are drawn together through time. In 'Lifting' (pp. 44–5), the wakes of the boats merge, are 'enwound', like the catch of eels, so that the paths of the individual boats cannot be isolated. And there is no way of saying when this whole process and way of life began, only the fisherman's reply can give a time, 'once the season's in'.

It is then a world preserved seasonally through time but it is also, like the wood in 'Up the Shore', hardened into stone. The very continuity and repetition through time of both eels and men, the men in their fatalism, the eels in their instinctive drives, become static responses. There is no way to break out from the lyric enclosure, from the intertwining imagery. Indeed, this intertwining technique lends itself to the economy of lyric more than to narrative. It impedes the onward flow of narrative. 'A Lough Neagh Sequence' is a sequence of lyrics, perceptions drawn from the life of the eel and the fishermen of Lough Neagh, rather than narrative or even the substitute for narrative that sequences often are, as for example a sequence which concentrates on the high dramatic moments and leaves out the bits setting up the plot. But in 'A Lough Neagh Sequence' that's not what Heaney is doing. Rather he seems more intent on examining a state of being than on any narrative sense. Movement here is repetition. Neil Corcoran offers one possible reading here when he speaks of the 'darker sexuality' of 'A Lough Neagh Sequence'. He goes on, a little less positively, to speak of it giving Heaney

> a weird and compelling subject – the life cycle of the eels and the work cycle of the fisherman on Lough Neagh – which may also act, as it moves through proverb, legend, realism and 'visionary' transmutation, as a kind of objective correlative for the compulsions of human sexuality.[3]

And in 'Vision', he finds 'something strained and portentous, as the passing of the eels across land is made slippery with adolescent sexual disgust'.[4] Does 'Vision' or the entire sequence give us leave to say this, either as a direct account of its meaning or as an inference from the contents?

My feeling is that such a reading offers too singular and limiting a response. Central as 'the compulsions of human sexuality' are to us, nonetheless the emphasis on historical continuity and tradition in the sequence seems to require a more inclusive reading. Tradition and history – I would argue – can tell us who we *were* but might prevent us from realizing who we *are*. It is odd that we could derive this thought essentially from Heaney's use of a certain kind of coalescing imagery. Lyric also predisposes poets to a form of rest. It subdues movement to rest. In Heaney, it seems to me, it is more a matter of allowing the two, rest and movement, to fulfil themselves simultaneously, to see 'wood' and 'stone' at the same time. Things preserved are still maintained in life. But the conflict is there and will not go away. What I think we can deduce about Heaney's habits of thought from all this is that he has an impulse to draw things together, to make one of the many. What we cannot be sure about and cannot specify beyond the particular instance is the outcome of that coalescing.

The structure of the self-reflexive image then cannot be seen as always specifying a particular meaning – psychological, sociological, aesthetic or whatever. If I can attempt a general statement about this type of image, it may be that its real virtue is to be a multi-purpose shape, an algebra, as it were, for conveying a meaning when it is invested with a content.

Language

Much as the use of a particular image structure in *Door into the Dark* led us to read and draw into a total argument a number of poems, so the question of Heaney's attitudes to language will lead us to read many poems, sorting through them for evidence. I put it this way because writers do not compartmentalize their thought in quite the way critics have to in chasing themes. Poems are built of many such themes, so that history, language, politics, land, religion, to take just a few pervasive Irish issues, are scarcely capable of being prised apart without loss and misrepresentation. As critics we do prise them apart but only to simplify complexity into clarity, the better to understand the complexity when we put things back together again, that is to say when we reread the poems.

In this spirit, then, I would like you to read all the poems from *Wintering Out* printed in *Selected Poems*, drawing out from them comments on the act of language itself. Then, return to two poems 'Anahorish' (p. 58) and 'Traditions' (pp. 68–9). And ask yourself two questions. What things are particularly associated with the Irish place-name – and Irish is here meant to indicate both the language and the country – Anahorish? And what is the relationship between Irish and English in 'Traditions'? You may find yourself asking two further questions. When Heaney speaks of languages, does he imply something or some things wider than the languages themselves? And why should Heaney be so bothered about the question anyway? *Wintering Out*, bear in mind, was published in 1972, his first book since leaving the North to live in the Irish Republic.

DISCUSSION

It does not always seem to register very strongly with non-Irish people that there is a distinct Irish language, distinct that is from English. It is a language of great antiquity, still current, expressive and sustained through fifteen centuries by a considerable literature, of course spoken in its various developments long before that.

Almost invariably, people outside Ireland will have never actually seen or heard any. Here then is a ninth-century poem called 'The Vikings', in Irish with an English translation by James Carney. I could equally have chosen a poem written yesterday.

> Is acher in gáith in-nocht,
> fu-fúasna fairggæ findfolt:
> ni ágor réimm mora minn
> dond láechraid lainn úa Lothlind.
>
> Bitter and wild is the wind to-night
> tossing the tresses of the sea to white.
> On such a night as this I feel at ease:
> fierce Northmen only course the quiet seas.[5]

We'll come back to the wider significance of language in Irish culture. But first let's look at what it signifies in 'Anahorish' and 'Traditions'. Anahorish is not simply a placename meaning 'place of clear water' but it is one of Heaney's own placenames, 'my' place. It is also an English transliteration for the original Irish sounds, not a name incorporating non-Irish elements. So in celebrating it he celebrates his Irish roots, his origins. It is then 'the first hill' associated with other beginnings, 'spring', 'bed', 'wells', 'dunghills', which are all points of source, of life and growth. The things that are observed are seen with the attentiveness, the closeness to the ground, of the child, another beginning, so the springs are seen as they wash into 'the shiny grass', and their waters darken the cobbles in the lane. But at the point from which the name 'Anahorish' is now observed it is not a present image, rather an 'after-image'. Constructed now in terms of an image of light, it is not the light directly received, but received as memory, a lingering on the retina, not in the physical sight, but in the mind. The same movement, from a physical present to a memory is used to take that memory, the lamps swinging through the farmyards of Heaney's childhood, back, by the archaeological suggestion of the word 'mound-dwellers', to the ancestral and original inhabitants of the hill. The poem then is an investigation into origins induced by the name of an Irish townland. Heaney describes that name in terms that intimately combine two elements, language, 'consonant', 'vowel', and land, 'gradient' and 'meadow'. Suffusing the whole poem is a gentleness and a sense of security, indicated at this point, both the heart and origin of the poem, by the word 'soft'. In the related poem 'Broagh', stimulated by another placename, another aspect of that security emerges. Its warmth depends on a degree of closeness and that closeness can exclude as well as include. And so in 'Broagh' the difficulty that strangers find in pronouncing the final '-gh' marks them as strangers, not intimates. The language then acts as a line of recognition, marking intimate from stranger, and coincides with a geography, a homeland for the 'mound-dwellers'. It acts, therefore, in political terms, in a literal as well as a metaphorical sense.

But the language he *writes* in, English, is, or may be seen as, culturally dissonant from the culture he inhabits, which is Irish, just as for a Scottish or Welsh, an American or Nigerian poet, English as a language may be seen as at odds with the culture for which he or she writes and speaks. In the nineteenth century, as a result of economic, political and penal pressures, combined with the depredations of famine and emigration which were particularly felt in Irish-speaking districts, the language was in retreat, though not defeated.[6] A number of pressures restored it. It did not, let it be said, need resurrecting but rehabilitating. The pressures were scholarly and antiquarian, literary and nationalist, social and religious. In religious terms, Protestant clergyman were often to the forefront, needing the language to convert an Irish-speaking Catholic population to Protestantism. In many of them, this became a disinterested concern with Irish culture. The poets gradually became aware of a wealth of indigenous mythology in the early Irish texts, rivalling the Greek in its range and excitement. Political journalists saw it as a means of national identification. Scholars saw this study of the language as a way in which they could contribute to that search for identity and align themselves with the residual Irish population which actually spoke it. The language can still act as a focus for Irish national consciousness.

Might Heaney then, be uneasy in his use of English as the medium for the intimate art of poetry? Well, certainly the question must be raised. As we'll see later in the final section of 'Station Island', he lets the spirit of James Joyce tell him roundly that 'the English language belongs to us'.[7] This implies, though, that Heaney has at least had to eliminate the question. And it is in 'Traditions' that he had signalled to himself how to do it. First he sketches the condition of language in Ireland. 'Long ago' the Irish language had been 'bulled' by English. 'The alliterative tradition' of poetry, inherited from Anglo-Saxon times and still current in the fourteenth century in England, is presumably used by Heaney to represent English as a language of consonants as contrasted with Irish, a language of vowels, the vowels 'guttural' sounding in mouth and throat, the consonants on the lips and teeth. The truth of this, as distinguishing the two languages, is questionable, but it affords a strong opposition for Heaney, which is what he needs. There is an interesting comment in Heaney's essay 'Feeling into Words' in *Preoccupations* bearing on this. He connects his own early attraction to Gerard Manley Hopkins with the Northern Irish accent, 'A staccato consonantal one'.[8] 'Long ago' has perhaps a suggestion that the question is past, the languages cannot be prised apart, but 'bulled' has an animal harshness suggesting force, rape and insemination. However inevitable and sanctioned by custom the resulting language has become, the circumstances of its development were invasion and occupation and that is still to be seen as violation. A similar ambivalence can be discerned in the second section of the poem. 'We are to be proud' for example, suggests another enforcement. It is not the same as 'we are proud'. At the most these 'archaisms' are 'cherished'. The accent too, 'the furled consonants', and its borrowed language 'bawn' and 'mossland' are all marks of the imperial thrust. MacMorris, the Irishman in *Henry V* is another victim, 'gallivanting' and whingeing in the poses of the stage-Irishman. He is especially sensitive about his 'nation':

> What ish my nation? Ish a villain, and a bastard,
> and a knave, and a rascal. What ish my nation?
> who talks of my nation?

But Bloom, in Joyce's *Ulysses*, has a shorter way with it. For him to be born here – the existential given of one's birth – settles the question of who one is. 'I was born here' he says, 'Ireland'. Heaney's remark in 'The Ministry of Fear' from *North*, that

> Ulster was British, but with no rights on
> The English lyric[9]

is a similar assertion that there are certain given conditions and for him, at least, the English language is his and not problematic. If in 'Traditions' Heaney asserts his nationality, we may equally see him as accepting the language in which he writes. Both are 'given'.

But there is a careful irony in Heaney's use of Bloom's words in 'Traditions'. To develop this I will have to move beyond the specific question of language into the continuities of Irish history, its past and its present. Bloom, you can take it, is giving what is Heaney's own reply. And Heaney, equally born in Ireland, is born in that part of it territorially British. He writes of the North and is impassioned with it. It is not just the English lyric where British rights are in question. And the use of the English language, of English publishers and of English markets is in no sense an acquiescence or sell-out as far as Heaney is concerned, however some people might see it so. The point here is that in many situations in the world, not least in Northern Ireland, a cultural statement is also a political one. Politics are the collective acts of people in pursuit of government and people use speech, sing songs, write poems. No statement is without its politics. It will be convenient here to sketch – no more than that – something of the Irish background to show why in the late 1960s and 1970s, when Heaney was first being published, politics will inevitably mark his concerns.

I will illustrate my sketch with reference to the poems 'Bog Oak' (pp. 56–7) and 'Servant Boy' (p. 59), and also to the dedicatory poem to *Wintering Out*, which is not in *Selected Poems*.[10] These poems between them range through Irish history up to the present. Do read the ones in *Selected Poems* and, also, to fill out a sense of language as a symbolic presence in Heaney's sensibility read 'Gifts of Rain' (pp. 63–5), 'Oracle' (p. 67) and 'A New Song' (p. 70).

The underlying structures of contemporary Northern Irish politics[11] were laid in the sixteenth century, from which time English and Scottish Protestant planters gradually established a monopoly of economic and political ascendancy over the Catholic and largely Gaelic majority who were already there. This ascendancy was echoed more largely by the economic and political control which England maintained and enforced over the whole island. The Protestant minority in Ireland expressed claims to Irish political independence as long as they remained in an untroubled ascendancy, but once the seeds of republican revolution, on the French model, were sown in Europe in the late-eighteenth century, the bulk of Protestants tended to seek their own furtherance in first accepting (1800) and then maintaining a union with Great Britain. Only in the north-east of Ireland did such a policy act seriously against the growing nationalist sentiment of the whole island. This division came to a head in the first two decades of this century, when the British government, in an attempt to satisfy, however reluctantly, both positions created a separate northern state, 'Northern Ireland', which comprised six of the nine counties of the historic northern Irish province of Ulster. This was to remain an integral part of the United Kingdom and was so constructed as to have a permanent Protestant majority, about two-thirds to one-third. The projected 'Southern Ireland', consisting of the remaining 26 counties and 94 per cent Catholic, became established, after a successful guerrilla war against the British, as the Irish Free State in 1921 and finally in 1949 as a sovereign Irish Republic. In so far as the territorial question has never been settled, as far as the Republic is concerned, and political and social justice for the minority has been deficient, to say the very least, in the North, this solution has never worked easily. Republicans campaigned sporadically in the North, between 1954 and 1958 for example, but the present campaign, virtually continuous since August 1969, had its origins not in any territorial claims nor in guerrilla action, but in a peaceful campaign for civil rights, largely relating to local government, housing and employment. It was inevitable, with the intervention of state and sectarian violence in breaking up the marches of 1968 and 1969, that the confrontation should form up in terms of traditional loyalties and aspirations. But the early tone was more ambitious than that. Civil rights envisaged a social revolution, not sectarian entrenchment. In a sense it was pragmatic, not simply fostered on old ideals. In the period leading up to the publication of *Wintering Out* such aims were savaged. In his dedicatory poem to the book, Heaney sees 'the new camp for the internees', fresh bomb craters and machine-guns, and all is 'déjà-vu, some film made of Stalag 17'. And he asks

> Is there a life before death? That's chalked up
> on a wall downtown. Competence with pain,
> coherent miseries, a bite and sup,
> we hug our little destiny again.
>
> (*Wintering Out*, p. 5, unnumbered)

What is at issue here, is whether pain is enough and whether the traditions aggrandize or demean the individual. 'Bog Oak', that toughened survival from the Irish past, which formerly would have been a standby for Heaney, leading him to his shared identity with the past, takes him back now, past 'hopeless wisdom' to a people who creep 'towards watercress and carrion' in the shattered Elizabethan landscape of Edmund Spenser, poet of *The Faerie Queene*, Lord Deputy of Ireland, and depressed author of a *View of the Present State of Ireland* (written 1595–96, published 1633). It is of course a new realization of the identity Heaney shares. The heroic is gone. Survival is all. Only so much as can be hugged close – 'our little destiny' – seems sustainable. Heaney's identity takes on elements less splendid than the diggers, pioneers and blacksmiths. In 'Servant Boy' he comes to terms with the role of so many Irish people in the past, of being, as the phrase is, 'in service' or 'hired'. But to come to terms with it entails giving it dignity.

> He is wintering out,
> the back-end of a bad year.

He may be 'a jobber among shadows' but he kept patience and counsel,

> . . . resentful
> and impenitent,
> carrying the warm eggs.
>
> (p. 59)

To conclude then, in *Wintering Out* a new and important centre of interest is articulated, language, in particular the Irish language. The implications of this concern are not simply literary. A concern for language is, obviously enough, always a distinguishing mark for the writer. It is the substance of the poet's skill. Language can be presented, at least theoretically as a world of its own, answering its own laws and having only a fortuitous connection with any exterior reality. It can be seen as determining structures rather than as representing them. As such it is a powerful reinforcing agent for the writer and, even more, in our day, for the critic. Heaney's interest in language can easily be presented as part of a general interest for writers, justifying and celebrating their own predilections, and then for critics, acolytes who, rapidly enough, become priests of the language craft. But this would be to misrepresent Heaney. His sense of language is grounded in the history and circumstances of his land.

Distancing

At the beginning of this chapter I said that I would deal with poems that we could group together, because they shared some common feature. This section will concentrate largely on 'The Tollund Man', but I hope it will be apparent that the implications of the discussion will have much wider reference to the body of Heaney's work. Towards the end I will explore a couple more poems and then indicate some others that bear fruitfully on the theme of 'distancing'.

One of the dangers of lyric poetry is that it is too easily formed in the autobiography of the poets. Moreover, where the poet does seek out feelings and events in other lives, they are simply remade as analogues and symbolic equivalents for prior preconceived interior feelings. I say this is a danger because I believe that what is interesting in a poet is not the documentation of an idiosyncratic or particular psyche – the poet's that is – but rather the poems. And those poems are to be seen as systems or shapes bringing into control and measure random experience. The poem is, in effect, a probe into the nature of being, winning structures from chaos. Obviously this can be done in terms of the individual psyche. 'The growth of a poet's mind' can provide the illuminating paradigm. And less portentously individual events in a poet's biography may strike chords and parallels in the lives of others. But there comes a point at which a *distance* is needed, an element akin to dramatic imagination, so that contemplation can displace self-analysis. It is in this spirit that I want you to read and think about Heaney's poem 'The Tollund Man', where a deliberate and discernible act of distancing occurs (pp. 78–9). By distancing I mean a standing-off, a removal from the interior preoccupations, in order to see things, including oneself, more clearly. There seem to me several devices – I'll call them that – which promote a sense of distancing in 'The Tollund Man'. What would you say they were? And to what degree, at the end of the poem, does Heaney bring the 'distancing' home to himself? And conversely can we see Heaney as being absorbed into the distances he has perceived? Finally, is there any way we should see this embracing of distance unsympathetically, as an evasion rather than a realization of identity?

DISCUSSION

I hope, first of all, the poem has been fairly clear to you at an immediate reading. 'The Tollund Man' is preserved at Aarhus, in Denmark. He was a victim in some ancient ritual dedicated to 'the goddess'. The body has been preserved in the peat by the 'dark juices' of the goddess's 'fen'. Heaney has not seen the man but says that one day he will go to see him. Probably from the precision of his description he's seen a photograph of it, though he doesn't say so. In the second section, using images of religion and of germination introduced earlier, the poet thinks that he might invoke the Tollund man to resurrect the flesh of labourers killed in an ambush, one surmises in Ireland. In the third section he anticipates that if he were to drive towards Aarhus something of the Tollund man's 'sad

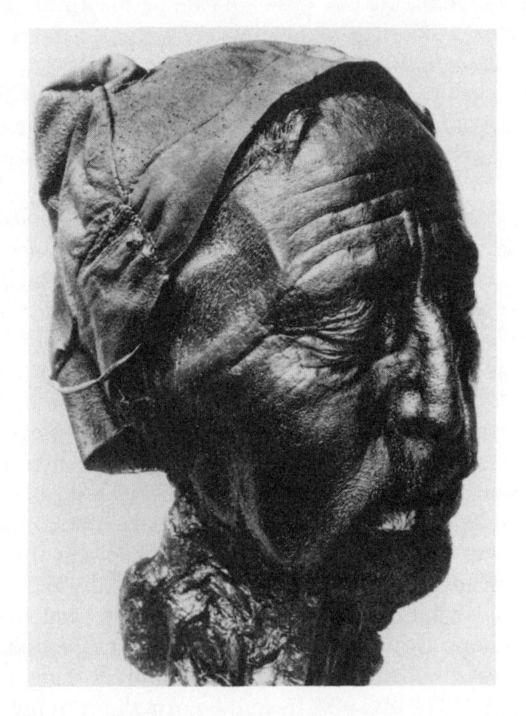

The Tollund Man, from P. V. Glob's *The Bog People*, where Heaney first came across 'his peat-brown head'.

freedom' would come to him. There, in Jutland, he 'will feel lost' and yet 'at home'.

I've started my account in this way because I think the poem gives all the information we need to see how it works and what it works towards. I make the point because so many discussions of the poem start from Heaney's own interesting commentary on it in his essay 'Feeling into Words' in *Preoccupations*. This refers us to a book, *The Bog People* by P. V. Glob, in which Heaney saw 'unforgettable photographs' of bodies preserved since the Iron Age in the Danish bogs.[12] They were of people sacrificed in a vegetation ritual to the Mother Goddess to ensure that the land would be renewed each spring. And Heaney, pondering images adequate to the situation in his own land, the North of Ireland, links these victims with more modern ones in Ireland. Heaney's account is, of course, useful comment on the way a poem gets written, and illuminates the poem's occasion, but it may in fact divert our attention from the poem itself. For Heaney to say that he was seeking images 'adequate to our predicament' explains why he is attracted to the photograph of the Tollund man, but still does not explain or delimit the poem he wrote. And his account is not at all where we *need* to start, but rather we should begin in the web of imagery he uses in the poem itself.

To the 'distancing' then. In the first line two kinds of distance are invoked, first of future time – 'I will go' – and second of geographical space – 'to Aarhus'. Then there are distances in the way we possibly can regard the Tollund man. While movingly human, 'mild', 'naked', yet he is alien, his head 'peat-brown' his eyelids 'pods', his face 'stained'. He is 'trove' rather than simply a body. Although his stomach still holds food and its potential for growth and life, 'seeds', nonetheless he is absorbed into the being of the divine, 'bridegroom to the goddess' worked on (and of course preserved) by her 'dark juices'. He is distanced too by his composure, as of sanctity, 'mild', 'saint's kept body', 'trove', 'reposes'. He is perfected in death. The past and future distances of time run upon the immeasurable distance of eternity. In the second section a hypothetical spiritual distance is invoked, that between blasphemy and one's acknowledged faith. As this is hypothetical, so too is the miraculous possibility that prayer to the Tollund man might resurrect the 'scattered' flesh of the dead labourers; and so a sequence of distances is invoked between the Tollund man, the dead labourers, and the living in general, perhaps Heaney in particular. And even the bodies, 'stockinged corpses', are dispersed, 'scattered', skin 'flecking' the railway tracks. Removed in this way from the normalities of life the bodies inhabit a distant surreal world. In the third section, Heaney constructs his hypothetical journey to the distant villages of Denmark and is separated from them not now by geographical space, but by language, 'Not knowing their tongue' and the alien names. 'Out there' is a phrase which contemplates an illimitable psychic space. 'Jutland' brings it back to a knowable yet still unknown geography. In that old heroic landscape, with its codes of honour and its feuding ethic – and the word 'parishes', rich with ancient ecclesiastical administration, emphasizes the distance – in such a landscape Heaney would feel 'lost', alienated, distanced, 'unhappy'. And yet because the distance is already interior and familiar he would feel 'at home'. The distancing can be seen as a measure of understanding and return. In the poems we have seen before – 'Digging', 'Bogland' and 'At a Potato Digging' – Heaney has asserted continuities with the past, and with a geography. And we have been able to assent to the assertion. It has seemed right that Heaney should see himself as a legitimate heir of those pasts. They became part of his autobiographical claims and his identity. To discover elsewhere a parallel for the peat-bogs, sacrifice, terror and a new note of alienation, and yet to perceive through that a new kindred is to find, in a single image, the distance he needs to see beyond his case.

The weapons Joyce chose to confront the condition of Ireland included 'exile', his own willed removal from the pressures of his country. Heaney had similarly removed from his native scene, the North, to the Irish Republic, in 1972 to live in Wicklow. Viewed autobiographically that plea for continued residence in the last line of the poem, 'at home', invites us to see there the possibilities of desertion. But beyond possible autobiographies, following the tracks of many distances in the structures of the poem, its words celebrate, give shape to, an uneasy home that we are all heir to. We see here not just the growth of a poet's mind, but a reaching out in that mind to the condition of those not so clearly his own. As an appendix to this we could read Heaney's poem 'Bye-Child' (pp. 91–2). There a mother keeps her illegitimate child hidden in a henhouse but fed morning and evening, and now, Heaney says of him

> . . . you speak at last
>
> With a remote mime
> Of something beyond patience,
> Your gaping wordless proof
> Of lunar distances
> Travelled beyond love.

This speech is not an ordinary speech but remotely sensed, from Heaney seeing a photograph of the boy. It is perhaps a necessary distance, the emotion and direct pain not crowding in, not unlike Wordsworth's 'emotion recollected in tranquillity'.[13] But these are not direct reactions to the poet's own experience. Rather they are emotions generated by other people's experience and demanding his response. It is as if identity is no longer a problem. Notice the words that establish various kinds of distance in these final lines of the poem, 'at last', 'remote', 'beyond patience', 'lunar distances', 'beyond love'. And this is 'proof', not through the poet's means, words, but 'wordless'. The best means – patience, love, words – that life seems to afford must be transcended, passed through, for even these are of the world and transient. And look at 'Westering' (pp. 94–5) another poem of distances. Heaney is in California, beneath a map of the moon, and thinking of that same moon 'the last night in Donegal'. A journey, 'a free fall', had begun on Good Friday and ended in Donegal. It starts then at the penitential climax of the church year, altars stripped 'and congregations bent / To the studded crucifix'. 'What nails' Heaney asks, 'dropped out that hour?' – nails, the instruments of pain, are lost on the journey as the roads unreel. Back in Ireland Heaney imagines

> . . . untroubled dust,
> A loosening gravity,
> Christ weighing by his hands.

What does this poem say? Does Heaney reconstruct, at a distance and helped by distance, an Ireland, released to him and understood, and a Christ, beyond crucifixion, compassionate in judgement? Or does he understand some freedom of his own, a release? From what constraints? Of place? Of Faith? Indeed what nails – and whose – dropped out that hour? Has he come through a season of winter, to the free fall of summer and beyond? Maybe so, but as with most good poems, the complexities of it all are held and, I suspect, stay in suspension.

In this chapter we have been looking at various aspects of poetic usage; a special type of imagery; language both as means and symbol; and distancing, a technique to carry the poet's contemplation beyond his own mind and its responses into the dramatic imagining of others. At the same time, each of these points of entry into the poems has uncovered links with other aspects of the poet's interest; history, politics, faith, the human condition. Poems have been seen as probes into the nature of being, winning structures from chaos and holding diverse, even opposed elements in suspension, their function not so much to resolve as to articulate, to give a place to things. The bye-child, confined in the henhouse 'was incapable of saying anything', Heaney tells us, and then leads him to speech.

Some other poems which focus such distances and bring home

other worlds to us and yet do not compromise the suffering or loneliness of those worlds are 'Maighdean Mara' (pp. 88–9) and 'Limbo' (p. 90). And for something quieter, more domestic, but with its own contemplated distance, 'Goodnight' (p. 93).

4. *North*

In 1975 Seamus Heaney published *North*. *Selected Poems* prints a good number of its poems, but *North* itself is less a collection of separate poems, than a carefully planned and unified book, with nothing out of place or diversionary. The effect resembles that of a painter exhibiting a series of thematically related pictures. The Northern theme is an inclusive one. The allusion is first to the North of Ireland but a large part of the content is, in fact, directed to a wider Northern myth, Viking society and its impact on and parallels with Ireland. This allows full play to the themes first raised in 'The Tollund Man' but those themes are augmented by a sense of a close, feuding, brutal yet joyous society. After the two dedicatory poems 'Sunlight' and 'The Seedcutters', the book is constructed in two parts. The first presents the Northern myth, incorporating archaeological, linguistic and sexual images already traced in *Wintering Out* and *Door into the Dark*. These are the images I have already examined in, for example 'The Tollund Man', 'Anahorish' and 'Undine'. In the second part, the actual conditions of the North of Ireland, as perceived by Heaney, are examined in poems as biting and colloquial as anything he has written.

But first the two dedicatory poems (pp. 98–100). They are written to Heaney's aunt Mary and they are important to the overall effect of *North*. In some sense they fall outside the massive concerns and anguishes of the whole book and instead celebrate a quietude. They calmly delineate domestic haven and ordinary custom. And yet there is more to them than simple realistic description of the everyday. Read 'Sunlight' and see if you can separate out from the description of concrete objects and physical actions any things we might class as abstractions. When you find them, think how they relate to the rest of the poem. Are they opposed to it, or complementary, or its summation?

DISCUSSION

The physicality of the body of the poem is easily seen, the iron pump described as 'helmeted', the 'honeyed' water, the bucket, and the sun 'like a griddle', 'the wall' of the afternoons, so that even the abstraction 'time' is given physical embodiment. All these come in the first 85 words. And yet the verse is light, not overloaded, uncannily lit by the first of Heaney's governing abstractions 'absence'. Any sense that the cascade of words, with the shapes and sensations it renders, is a clutter is disarmed by this controlling word 'absence'. The sum of all this endeavour is a relished emptiness, something indeed to be filled, but already somehow radiant and fulfilled. Absence is not a negative condition here. Nor is it like a vacuum, potential and inviting inrush. It is rather as if things aspire upwards to a transfigured and emptied condition which expresses them totally. And in the second element of the poem, prefaced by 'so', Heaney runs a similar sequence, this time his aunt, making bread. He visualizes her, and the work she does, intensely, 'hands', 'bakeboard', 'reddening stove' and so on. Even the heat of the stove is given physicality by the word 'plaque'. And all this physical filling of our minds ends with another abstraction, 'here is a space / again'. How space differs from the way Heaney has already used 'absence' is not easy to define. I have already suggested that 'absence' was in no way negative but perhaps 'a space' is even more clearly positive. It is a location, a place to be, to move and to breathe. And here, in this kitchen scene, Heaney concludes, is 'love' and clinches the way in which 'love', though an abstract quality, can only be humanly rendered in the ordinary actions of life.

> . . . love
> like a tinsmith's scoop
> sunk past its gleam
> in the meal-bin.

This consonance between the abstract idealized quality and its practical and physical placing is of the utmost importance for the world that Heaney's poetry strives to locate. And that is why it is placed here to open *North*, a book trying to control and shape the agonized dissonances of the north of Ireland. In her book *all of us there*, Polly Devlin quotes her sister, Heaney's wife, talking about the family he grew up in.

> . . . I discovered my husband didn't have this sense of loss, this feeling of being left behind. He thinks if a place is empty then he's the first there . . . His family life was utterly together like an egg contained within the shell, without any quality of otherness, without the sense of loss that this otherness brings.[1]

In the light of this it might be sensible to think of Heaney's searchings and apparent pursuit of identity within the conflicting calls of art and life, north and south and so on, more as acts of restoration rather than search, as efforts to reconstruct something known, to relocate 'a space'.

Polly Devlin's title *all of us there* is taken from the second of these dedicatory poems, 'The Seed Cutters'. She speaks of the words working 'their stealth' on her.[2] Presumably she thought that, unsensational as it might appear, the phrase epitomized a community. Heaney mentions the painter Brueghel in his poem and 'The Seed Cutters' is indeed like a picture that Brueghel might have painted. Heaney is not the first twentieth-century poet to be attracted to qualities in Brueghel. The American poet William Carlos Williams constructed an impressive sequence 'Pictures from Brueghel'[3] from looking at, describing and quietly commenting on a number of Brueghel's paintings and, earlier still, W. H. Auden centred his 'Musée des Beaux Arts'[4] on Brueghel's *The Fall of Icarus*. So Brueghel has been a fruitful source but Heaney is unusual in proposing a picture for Brueghel to paint. Read 'The Seed Cutters' (p. 100). Can you see any good reason why Heaney should set up his poem as a sort of conversation with Brueghel? You could, in approaching that question, think about the phrase 'compose the frieze' as a help to you. And then why do you suppose Heaney talks of 'our anonymities'? Is he undercutting the life of the society he depicts? Or celebrating it?

DISCUSSION

I think Brueghel might serve three functions in the poem. First he gives a visual anchor, a style if you like, for Heaney's own description. He tells us in other words that the seed cutters look like one of Brueghel's pictures, a piece of information which gives us an easy way in to the poem's visual effects. This is, of course, assuming we've seen some of Brueghel's pictures already. If he had started the poem at line 3 he would have had a slightly tougher time getting the overall scene to cohere in our minds. This in turn would mean that the close-up, the crucial detail of the poem, the visualization of the cut potato, gleaming and with its dark watermark at the centre, would not so clearly act as a repeating and unchanging summation of the workers' life – simply because he had not already visualized them as framed, singular and coherent.

Secondly, Brueghel, being an 'Old Master', conveniently allows Heaney to extend the lives of his seed cutters back in time. If Brueghel will 'know' them, then they must have existed at least potentially in Brueghel's own time. And, Heaney does say 'They seem hundreds of years away'. So Brueghel gives Heaney yet another way of establishing a link with his imagined ancestors.

Finally Brueghel functions as another artist, facing with Heaney the problems that artists do, of presenting a view of the real, of translating raw and momentary experience into stability whether as painting or poem. Here we seem to overhear a conversation between two artists, one explaining to the other an idea for a picture. Heaney gives himself a means not to address us directly, which is a great way to deflect lyric from being merely personal statement. So Heaney suggests that Brueghel should 'compose the frieze', the sequence of figures that makes up the scene and epitomizes man's recurrent seasonal pattern of activity. Life becomes art: art savours life and 'all of us' are 'there'. And now the conclusion, 'our anonymities', which is so skilful and so exact as, at least for me, to strike wonder. To be anonymous is, for most of us, no great compliment. We strive to be individual, to be known and recognized. We are exhorted to 'be somebody'. We pursue fame or notoriety and admire those who achieve it. And yet, in final terms, we are mostly anonymous, not attended by obituaries in *The Times*, barely mentioned in the local paper. Undeniably though, we are all real and our degree of reality is absolute, not conditional upon our degree of fame, nor overridden by our anonymity. Indeed it is our anonymity, not needing to strut an hour upon a stage, that confirms the absoluteness of our reality, since all have it equally, not earned but given. Anonymity makes us one, composes us in the one frame with everybody else, stretched across generations and countries and mediated by the vision of diverse artists. It is a realization that does not depersonalize us but gives us our full reality. Heaney recognizes it in Brueghel's figures, in his own seed cutters and in himself. 'All of us' are there. It is an important statement at the beginning of *North*, importantly placed.

Now to Part I of the book. In my discussion of 'The Tollund Man' I was offering the view that it uses devices for distancing Heaney from the Northern 'predicament'. In an interview with Brian Donnelly in 1977 he suggested that, in contemplating the events of the North in all their numbing and immediate effect, words 'become inert', rather than realize themselves as poems. Instead he found his poetic energies quickened by the 2000-year-old victims of the Earth goddess,

> And it was in these victims made strangely beautiful by the process of lying in bogs that somehow I felt I could make offerings or images that were emblems.[5]

In the first part of *North* this process of subsuming contemporary Northern Irish events in coherent and completed memorial artistic acts is carried much further. Heaney no longer sees the Scandinavian peoples as far away parallels but invites them home. Historically, the Vikings invaded Ireland. That's what the medieval Irish poem on p. 41 was about. They founded many of the country's larger settlements and left their mark in its placenames. In Dublin, Viking archaeological sites were being minutely examined even as Heaney wrote. In *North* Heaney embraces the invaders and so adds another layer to Irish ancestry.

I want you now to read 'Funeral Rites' (pp. 101–4). Notice the way Heaney again mixes ancient with modern deaths by violence. What does the phrase 'each neighbourly murder' mean, and what do you think of it? Bearing in mind the violence in the North of Ireland since 1969, what do you think of Heaney's desire for ceremony? And does ceremony imply celebration and ratification?

DISCUSSION

In 'Funeral Rites' Heaney grows to maturity, 'stepping in to lift the coffins of dead relations'. It is all given ceremony, the laying out, the rosary, candles and the 'black glacier of each funeral'. It is as well to say here that in Ireland funerals are much more collective acts of reassurance and communal solidarity than they tend to be in England. It is not that they are not sad, but that the whole structure of belief tends genuinely to spread the net of grief and to widen the range of consolation. Heaney has, as always, as most of us have at funerals, a degree of detachment, noticing the hands 'shackled in rosary beads' and himself kneeling 'courteously / admiring it all'. But mere observation is shattered and distance annihilated by the simple ordinariness of the adjective 'dear' in 'dear soapstone masks' to describe the faces of the dead. The style and the mind that creates the style are very lithe. 'Each neighbourly murder' is another phrase of this kind. It is not just or even primarily ironic. You could call it grim, but it is also exact. It has the note of intimacy, the common understanding of a code of behaviour. What is missing here is normal ceremony. The ambushes, the shootings are too many, too successive to wait on the 'temperate' tread of the cortège past the homes, with their blinds drawn. Heaney would prescribe a massive ceremonial cortège of cars headed in 'slow triumph' to the great Neolithic chambered tombs on the River Boyne, at various sites, but notably

Newgrange in County Meath. The serpent imagery used to describe the procession echoes the spiral carving on the stones there. In the drive back north, Strangford and Carlingford Loughs will be restored to their Viking etymologies and pasts and the mourners.

> the cud of memory
> allayed for once, arbitration
> of the feud placated,

would imagine the buried disposed like Gunnar, the Norse hero in the *Volsungsaga*, who 'dead by violence / and unavenged' yet chanted 'verses about honour'. The tomb opened 'as he turned / with a joyful face / to look at the moon'. It is a mass elegy, neither condemnatory, nor analytic. It simply commemorates and recognizes an ancient heroic parallel of 'honour' and joyousness in heroic death. The whole strife has become an artefact, in a way. Is there more that, as a poet, Heaney could or should do? Yeats excluded Wilfred Owen from his *Oxford Book of Modern Verse* (1936), along with other World War One poets, 'because they felt bound . . . to plead the sufferings of their men' and it was Yeats's view that passive suffering is not a theme for poetry.

Inside Newgrange, one of the burial 'chambers of Boyne', last resting place in the ceremonies of 'Funeral Rites'. Looking towards 'the megalithic doorway'.

> In all the great tragedies, tragedy is a joy to the man who dies; in Greece the tragic chorus danced, when man has withdrawn into the quicksilver at the back of the mirror no great event becomes luminous in his mind; it is no longer possible to write *The Persians*, *Agincourt*, *Chevy Chase*: some blunderer has driven his car on to the wrong side of the road – that is all.[6]

Yeats is also recorded as saying that the creative man must impose himself upon suffering, as he must also upon Nature.

It is in the light of thinking of this kind that Heaney's transfigured view of the neighbourly murders should be seen. All his preparations for the massive cortège are conceived as fitting recognition for sacrificed lives. In 'Easter 1916' Yeats answered his own dilemma about the leaders of the Rising:

> We know their dream; enough
> To know they dreamed and are dead.[7]

In both cases it is a recognition of the reality of the deaths rather than the ratification of the causes. Again the final account of Gunnar is by report: 'Men said'. What Heaney perceives is that it is possible for these events to be seen in such a way. The transformation is possible and it is his function as poet to see it as possible.

In a curious way the poet's statement is elevated above his own particular opinions about 'neighbourly murders' – opinions which are not stated. He becomes instead a mouthpiece for the loss. In this way he fills a void and he fills it with celebration, not of acts but of people. It is an alignment with the story-telling, celebratory and affirmative world that is reflected in the memorial words 'men said'.

Now read the title-poem 'North' (pp. 105–6). In it Heaney receives a message from the Viking raiders. What do they tell him in the last five stanzas, first about the circumstances of warfare and secondly about a possible response? Do you see this poem as setting up an analogy for the current state of the North and proposing a course of action for Heaney himself?

DISCUSSION

'North' examines, in the hindsight of history, the realities that pushed the Vikings, 'those fabulous raiders' on to their violent achievements. Their voices warn, 'lifted again in violence and epiphany'. Behind it all is 'geography and trade', and crude and envious politics. Peace, should it come, is not so much achievement as exhaustion. The recourse from this, the voice of 'the longship's swimming tongue' says, is to 'lie down in the word hoard' . . . 'compose in darkness'. Expect only the spread luminosity of the northern lights, nothing sensational, no visionary pyrotechnics. Trust what you know. This, then, is another reason for the artefact-like atmosphere of these poems. They are like relics or grave-goods, salvaged by the mind from the savagery of the times. Heaney establishes a voice for the passive observer as against the active or political or military roles that seem to be central. All seems to be vitiated, merely 'secular powers', 'unmagical invitations', and 'pathetic colonies'. The 'fabulous raiders' and the poet composing in darkness cannot but be set within this, but they can, by the fling of their exploits or their words, produce effects more splendid than their causes.

It would be too narrowing, too particularizing to see these 'Viking' poems, as simply justifying Heaney's sense of a role and drawing their strength from the complexity of the position he finds himself in. He lives and expresses the condition of the state, rather than backs off from it into isolation because it is all too much for him. But these are more than statements of political consciousness. In effect he is defining the nature of poems, expressing their peculiar mid-role between an external reality, which they engage, and a new and independently realized poetic world which manifests and obeys other laws. We are not concerned only with statements about life but about art, as a composing element in life. With an eye to this sense of art – of artefact – I would like you now to look at 'The Grauballe Man' (pp. 114–15) and to compare it with 'The Tollund Man'. In what ways are the poems different? And look closely at the method of description Heaney habitually uses in 'The Grauballe Man'. Is it different from 'The Tollund Man'? Remember our discussion of self-reflexive imagery in 'A Lough Neagh Sequence'? Is there anything similar here?

DISCUSSION

'The Grauballe Man', like 'The Tollund Man' is another meditation on the preserved corpse of a Scandinavian victim dug up from the peat-bogs. But where 'The Tollund Man' was concerned to draw a parallel between an Irish present and a Danish past and to affirm something from that kinship, the emphasis in 'The Grauballe Man' is different. Essentially the poem is about different ways of regarding corpses. The poem starts, unusually for Heaney, with a series of descriptions which are set up as similes and not metaphors, that is they use the devices 'as if', 'as', or 'like' to connect the thing described with the element used to describe. In metaphor the thing described is spoken of directly in terms of the element which is used as comparison. It is the difference between 'the grain of his wrists is like bog oak' (simile) and 'his hips are the ridge and purse of a mussel' (metaphor). These really are different phases of the linking process which is description. In simile, difference is recognized and so comparison is possible; in metaphor, an identity, at least in the possibilities present to language, is established and difference, again at the level of language, recedes. That is to say, in 'the grain of his wrists is like bog oak', we recognize a fact in life, that one thing may, indeed, look like another. In 'his hips are the ridge and purse of a mussel', we recognize a fact in art, that language can assert identities even where difference appears in life. This is the difference between thinking in categories, where we relate things to one another by gradations of difference and symbolic thinking where we relate things to one another by establishing an identity between them. Heaney is more inclined to this second mode than to the simile, but 'The Grauballe Man' begins with simile, carefully repeated, and only then moves to metaphor. Consider Heaney contemplating the corpse. How does his poem respond to the sight? The man – for it is a man Heaney sees, not a corpse, a presence rather than a non-existence – is 'as if he had been poured in tar', and 'seems to weep the black river of himself'. These things are not so, but the comparisons visually, and as an index of emotion, are valid.

The man is solid or better, solidified. Notice Heaney's interest in conditions which, once fluid, are now solid. Of course, where the two terms, of fluidity and solidity, are used close together in a poem, the effect is that both terms apply and so the object described resolves or, at least, contains the two opposites. Tar is therefore understood as having been poured and now as solidified. Similarly the river is, by nature, a permanent object but because it is always flowing, never the same. 'You cannot step in the same river twice', said Heraclitus. The river that is himself is created by the Grauballe man's own weeping. Or seems to be. 'Seems' is another 'like' word. Again notice Heaney's concern for self-reflexive imagery. Here, though, the self-reflexion is not an assertion of identity. Consider the difference had he written 'weeps the black river of himself'. This functions as a self-creating image, fully asserted, in which there is no sense that the action is observed or created from outside, by us as onlookers. The action does not promote an interaction between us and it. It is self-perfecting. Add 'seems', as Heaney does, and the action of self-creation, if indeed it takes place, is both observed from outside, and evidently produced by the observer, in so far as it is the poet as observer who draws attention to his own creation of the image. It draws our attention to the observer who said it, that is, the poet. Between these two 'like' constructions is a more certain, less subjective statement, the metaphorical 'he lies / on a pillow of turf', which acts in the poem to stabilize the movement and variables around it. Stability is, of course, the intended sense here. This is a nice example of a grammatical construction precisely complementing the wider sense that the statement implies. One further point should be made. We know there is a corpse here and can readily infer that it could be described directly in terms of measurement, weight, objectively accounted appearance and so on. The fact that such a description is not given, but may be inferred as a necessary base line, means that the 'as if' descriptions effectively produce a double image – an implied reality and a stated imaginative understanding. The effect is to create from a single object a new, laminated reality – which is of course, still a recreation of the corpse. In the poem, this laminating process will continue as the poem constructs itself. Immediately four such layered views are added, descriptive of various parts of the body, 'like bog oak', 'like a basalt egg', 'cold as a swan's foot', or 'a wet swamp root'. These are natural phenomena, preserved wood; stone but seen as egg-like; part of a living creature but cold rather than warm; a root, sign of life, but again by implication cold ('wet').

Each description extends our sense of the corpse, by involving it with aspects of a wider life and landscape but also each is itself a conjunction between the warmth and growth of life and of some sort of fixity, cold, stone, preserved. We see the corpse through a succession of superimposed filters or tracings, each adding something to a total and composite view. Heaney now tightens the process by moving from simile to metaphor, from his imagination, to the poem's assertion of the corpse's reality, '*are* the ridge', '*is* a visor'. The oppositional combining phrases continue, 'an eel arrested', 'the cured wound'. The corpse is a repository of many possible views but now also of a single reality. Our concentration is pointed to the wound which 'opens inwards to a dark / elderberry place'. Where else would Heaney's point of revelation be placed but in an inward-opening darkness? And indeed, in the strategies of *North*, where else but in a 'cruel wound', even if, perhaps especially if, it is arrived at by wordplay?

And the revelation is this – that we have something that no available word could refer to. We cannot name this sight. 'Who will say "corpse"?' . . . 'who will say "body"?' Its hair, old as it is, 'rusted', is like the hair of the yet unborn. Next we have a surprising move. After the vivid, layered meditation on the corpse, he says that he first saw the face in a photograph and now sees the whole corpse in memory. Neither is an actual sight then, understood as happening in the here and now of the poem. These are additional fusions in the reality the poem has constructed, though the one that comes closest to summing up the fusion is 'memory' – 'perfected in my memory'. It is not, of course, adequate because the poem which is, in effect, all the account we have, is not in memory but rather an enactment of memory. Its interrelationships are possible only to states like memory, dream, imagination, but its enactment can only become actual as the poem we have, different in kind therefore from the elements which construct it, but intimately related to them, because it is our deepest, most subtle access to them. The body so constructed is again a complex of opposites, 'hung in the scales / with beauty and atrocity'. These opposites, like 'the cured wound' are its substance, its determinants. Heaney expands 'beauty' to 'the Dying Gaul', the classical statue, Graeco-Roman tribute to the heroism of a Northern people, his fine but collapsed body unable to rise to its feet, and here 'too strictly compassed', by an art deployed on a functional military object, a shield. He expands 'atrocity', to his own time, and to all others, where hooded victims are 'slashed and dumped'. This is how a poem enters into human agony, certainly by saying how it is, but more by laying bare reading after reading of the event it memorializes until the unavailable word that is sufficient to it, is only just unuttered.

I want now to introduce a question which has been raised in critical discussion of Seamus Heaney's work, and especially by *North*. I mentioned it briefy in discussing 'Traditions'. The question relates to the 'politics' of the poems. Slightly more in sorrow than in anger, some critics feel worried about what they perceive to be 'Nationalist', 'Catholic', 'Republican' attitudes in them. Thus Blake Morrison writes in *British Poetry since 1970* (published 1980),

> It would be going too far to suggest that 'Punishment' in particular and the Bog poems generally offer a defence of Republicanism; but they are a form of 'explanation'. Indeed the whole procedure of *North* is such as to give sectarian killing in Ulster a historical respectability which it is not usually given in day-to-day journalism.[8]

Now it would seem reasonable to me that somebody, whether poet or not, should attempt an 'explanation' of acts such as both Republicans and Loyalists have committed in the North of Ireland. Explanation might help to end them. Further, to explain them does not imply giving 'historical respectability' to those acts, only historical context. I'm not sure what the judgements of 'day-to-day journalism' have to do with it since it's impossible to form a consensus of attitude from those day-to-day pronouncements. Some journalists clearly do look for historical understanding as Heaney does. Some are violently outraged and only that. Perhaps Morrison is making the point that Heaney is doing something different from making 'day-to-day' comment. He is attempting the long view. And so, his account is necessarily different from the immediate reactions of journalism. Whatever Morrison intends, though, 'respectability' is not what Heaney sees in acts of violence or wishes to give them.

Interestingly Blake Morrison, in a very good account of *North* in his book *Seamus Heaney*, written a year later (1981), revises the first sentence of the passage I have quoted. He doesn't say 'it would be going too far' to suggest that Heaney was offering 'a defence of Republicanism' but that, so powerful are the ancestral drives, we can really absolve him of responsibility for writing the poems.

> . . . one feels that Heaney is not writing his poems, but having them written for him, his frieze composed almost in spite of him by the 'anonymities' of race and religion.[9]

However, he speaks of Heaney showing 'the tribal prejudices of an Irish Catholic' and says in commenting on Heaney's poem 'Act of Union', that 'it is a mark of his race and religion that he should lay the blame where he does'.[10] But it might just be that he's right, 'a mark' of straight thinking. Morrison's expressions here, though sanctioned by the myths present in the poems and in common usage, have themselves taken an edge from a certain kind of day-to-day journalism. It is difficult to be quite judicious in the distinctions that have to be drawn. Edna Longley, more embroiled, in that she lives in the North of Ireland, speaks of the poem 'Kinship' (pp. 119–24) defining 'the battlefield in astonishingly introverted Catholic and Nationalist terms'[11] and, again, of 'The Tollund Man' she asks, 'has tribal pre-ordination, or ordination, any petrifying effect on poetic life?'[12] To which we are expected to answer, 'yes'. Now I think what is operating in views of this kind, is a concealed politics – though one that would disclaim politics – which would blame Heaney for being wrong, coupled with a sense of regret, because good poets like Heaney shouldn't be wrong. This leads to a further stricture that good poetry shouldn't be political and its mirror image, 'political' poetry isn't good. This is, in fact, more or less the declared position of Edna Longley. She writes:

> Poetry and politics, like church and state, should be separated. And for the same reasons: mysteries distort the rational processes which ideally prevail in social relations; while ideologies confiscate the poets' special passport to *terra incognita*. Its literary streak, indeed, helps to make Irish Nationalism more a theology than an ideology. Conor Cruise O'Brien calls 'the area where literature and politics overlap' an 'unhealthy intersection'; because, 'suffused with romanticism', it breeds bad politics – Fascism and Nationalism. But it also breeds bad literature, particularly, bad poetry, which in a vicious circle breeds – or inbreeds – bad politics.[13]

I really have only two questions to ask you. Do you agree that poetry and politics should be separated? If so, why? I am concerned here that you analyse the critical statements I have quoted as carefully as you look at the poems. Please now read 'Punishment' (pp. 116–17), 'Kinship' (pp. 119–24) and 'Act of Union' (pp. 125–6), and then consider them in the light of the above comments.

DISCUSSION

I should say first that though I have presented this as a question raised by two literary critics, it is a question that, as it were, Heaney first thought of. The pressures from the pain of Northern events seem overwhelming. If we are looking for confessional poetry, it would be hard to equal the last four stanzas of 'Punishment'. And why is Edna Longley astonished that Heaney, born into a Catholic Nationalist environment, when confronted with what he understandably sees as the continuing degradation of his own people through the due processes of the state, should express himself in the habitual images of those people? Those images have not been rendered invalid by the Troubles, only confirmed. In terms of the distancing that his address to Tacitus in 'Kinship' permits him, it is not unreasonable to say

> Our mother ground
> is sour with the blood
> of her faithful,
>
> they lie gargling
> in her sacred heart
> as the legions stare
> from the ramparts.

In the island, as Heaney sees it 'nothing will suffice'. He echoes Yeats's line from 'Easter 1916', about the deaths of the leaders of the Easter Rising, 'O when may it suffice?'.[14] Indeed Heaney's 'nothing' screws up the felt agony of it to a pitch beyond Yeats's. And Heaney too, expresses the exhaustion of the whole process.

> report us fairly,
> how we slaughter
> for the common good
>
> and shave the heads
> of the notorious,
> how the goddess swallows
> our love and terror.

If this is 'politics', with the pejorative edge that Longley seems to give the word, then the North could use a few such politicians. The words have an appeal to candour ('report us fairly'), a distaste for the camouflaging of act and policy in formulae ('how we slaughter/for the common good'), and precise insight ('how the goddess swallows/ our love and terror'). There is no way this is 'bad poetry' and I find it hard to think, among the political utterances in the North and at Westminster, that fair and exact speaking should be felt as 'bad' politics.

I suggested earlier that there is a concealed politics in Longley's position. I don't want to present hers as a sophisticated parallel to *The Protestant Telegraph* which saw Heaney as 'the well-known Papish propagandist' in 1972 when he moved South. No, this is much more a politics based on disappointment – that something that had seemed possible has now been lost. She writes:

> Yet one of the junctures where the North may harbour a cultural vanguard as well as a rearguard is the point where traditions meet and fuse in poetry. Early in the 1960s, not for the first time though more intensely than before, political confrontation – as during the Irish Literary Revival – turned into cultural encounter. Contraries no longer found in the South became progressive instead of regressive, and even adumbrated genuine unity. Within that space, for instance, the 'slightly aggravated young Catholic male' in Seamus Heaney was submerged by his urge to express 'the private county Derry childhood part of myself'.[15]

What Longley seems to ignore is that while 'the private county Derry childhood part' may be attractive – and to more people – it is not more authentic nor more legitimate than the religious and nationalist impulses. And further, to seek their elimination is precisely to deny the grounds of a meeting and a fusing of the traditions. What she says is in no way apolitical. It is politicized and it expresses the politics of disappointment, and so do Heaney's poems. Although I think Heaney is more clearsighted and more candid than Longley, I cannot think that his statements are less politicized. By politicized I mean, not 'propagandist' nor 'factional' but 'awake to the political condition'. Action within any state, any political entity, is inevitably political. And the same is true of inaction. In consequence Longley's plea that poetry and politics should be separate is impossible, indeed undesirable. It would exclude poets from writing about unemployment, poverty, oppression, war, all political questions. It is specious to identify poems as 'mysteries' that 'distort' when they are involved with political questions. And it is naïve to think that because 'rational processes' should ideally 'prevail in social relations' they habitually, in fact, do. The saner voices, visionary if not practical, are as often among the writers. Whether or not ideologies confiscate the poet's passport to the unknown really depends on the way the poet responds to the ideology. And ideology, in practice, can accommodate individual modification and the insight of imagination without its broad consensus being infringed. And whatever about the designation of Irish Nationalism as theology rather than ideology – and this looks a bit cheap to me – the same is, in fact, true of theology. As a mode of investigation much preoccupied with *terra incognita* it regularly accommodates the play of imagination and of individual insight. Otherwise Dante, Langland and Milton would not have emerged from their various catechisms, their poetry as intact as their faiths. The suggestion that the 'unhealthy intersection' of politics and literature breeds Fascism and Nationalism is curious, even if we limit its reference to Ireland. Could it not also 'breed' – loaded word – Communism, Anarchism, even Democracy, depending entirely on the politics and the circumstances of the writer? Also if Fascism is used at all precisely, it is used quite illicitly in the discussion here. If it isn't used precisely then it shouldn't be used at all. Heaney's poetry might appeal to traditional Irish Nationalists (as if Unionists aren't equally Nationalist – different nation). But living as I do in an English city where the National Front and the Orange Order recently both arrived to celebrate William of Orange's 1688 landing in England doesn't make me feel confident in the use of the word 'fascist' as a stick to locate or to beat, however more-in-sorrow-than-in-anger, Seamus Heaney or indeed any other Nationalistically inclined Northern poet. If what is meant is 'hard men', 'para-militaries', 'terrorists', that should be said and this different assertion proved.

What I have been doing here is to subject a persuasive piece of critical writing to the same sort of analysis as we have been applying to the poems we have discussed. I have tried to establish what it is really saying. Criticism, if it is not simply inert, is as committed as poetic expression. It constructs myths and fictions just as much, though it often suggests that it does not. Criticism should respect and describe the range of preferences that it meets in the poem before it subjects it to a grid of preferences imported from the critic's own stock of them. I don't think the piece I have analysed nor the book from which I have taken it does do that.

If we are looking for 'political' poems then Part II of *North* speaks with a satiric bite that has not shown itself in Heaney's writing up to this point. The bite is strongest in 'Singing School' (pp. 129–36), a sequence of memories and occasions which are seen as tutorial to Heaney's development as a writer. The title, already pleasantly ironic, is taken from Yeats's 'Sailing to Byzantium'. Yeats's 'singing school' for poets is 'monuments of its own magnificence' – great poems.[16] Heaney's titles like 'Ministry of Fear', 'A Constable Calls', 'Orange Drums, Tyrone, 1966' (not in *Selected Poems*), indicate a rougher kind of schooling. Central to a great deal of Heaney's day-to-day experience in the North of Ireland was a sense of opposed values, confronting or uneasily living with one another. These titles indicate that. And so too, this structure of opposition has its analogue in at least some of the poems.

Poets often use opposites to set, as it were, the widest limits on what the poem contains. The middle ground is contained though it may be in abeyance. Poetry is a most economic form of expression. And this liking for presenting opposites and holding them in the same limited space, to work one on another, is part of this economic instinct. Indeed when the opposites, through the procedures of paradox or pun or of some larger view, are seen to resolve, as I suggest they do in 'The Grauballe Man', then the pursuit of economy is even more rewarding.

A consequence of this poetic habit is that some poems, at least, can be conveniently described and analysed through observing the oppositions they contain. By tabulating the oppositions we can make clear the underlying structure of meaning the poem presents. 'A Constable Calls' (pp. 132–3) is one of Heaney's poems that can be treated in this way. Read it and see if you can see any clear line of opposition in the words used. Tabulate the words that seem to you to carry the poem's meaning and events most clearly. We might not come up with identical lists and we might indeed argue about where to place some of the words. Quite a few will stubbornly refuse to be coerced and marshalled in this way, but nonetheless a tendency towards forming two opposing groups of words should emerge. When you've got them listed, see what conclusions you might be able to draw from the opposition you have found.

DISCUSSION

I came up with two sets of words. Roughly there's one set to do with law, measurement and repression and another, much smaller, of crops to which the law is applied. My law, measurement and repression list would be 'treads', 'boot', 'law', 'line', 'pressure', 'bevel', 'unstrapped', 'ledger', 'acres', 'roods', 'perches', 'arithmetic', 'fear', 'holster', 'buttoned', 'cord', 'revolver butt', 'guilts', 'black hole', 'barracks', 'belt', 'domesday book', 'snapping', 'ledger', and 'boot' again.

You might reasonably object that's more or less the whole poem and certainly the preponderant atmosphere of the poem is of a child's fear of the law, its ministers and its pressures. And of course once we have set up this sinister set, other words, without such a load, are drawn to it. 'Cocked back', 'rubber', 'fat', 'black', 'sweating' reinforce a sense of interrogation and threat. The 'carrier spring' snaps like a man-trap. The constable puts his cap on, not nonchalantly with one hand, but exactly, with two. It is all now Heaney's loaded observation. And what is there to offer against it? Well, in numerical weight, not much. Only the things which are subject to this law, 'root crops', 'mangolds', 'marrowstems', and, of course, 'my father' and the 'staring' Heaney. And just as in 'The Other Side' there is a contrast between the firm order of the neighbour's land and the waywardness of Heaney's own, so here there is 'a line / Of turnips where the seed ran out / In the potato field', which his father doesn't mention. Now we know, I think, that neither Heaney's father nor the constable would be too bothered about this. Grown-ups are like that, but the child assumes 'small guilts'. Only later, I suspect, as an adult, can Heaney see these guilts as 'small'. At the time they are gross. 'Assumed' is a great word. One sense it has here is 'to take for granted' with the suggestion that to do so is not quite thought out. The assumption may be wrong. But another sense is 'to take upon oneself' as in 'he assumed the throne'. The young Heaney is here the willing sacrifice, taking upon himself a share in his family's 'guilt' before a repressive law. And notice Heaney's mental process in all this. He sat 'imagining'. Although the imaginings are horrific, nonetheless his mental mode is opposed to the measurement, 'the heavy ledger', the constable represents and his father acquiesces in, 'making tillage returns'. There are some other dissident elements here too. The credentials of the bicycle must be suspect, as it stands outside the action 'at the window-sill', its pedals 'relieved', 'Hanging' is good enough for them. And the dynamo's mechanism is called colloquially 'the spud', aligning it with the mythic centre of Irish rural life, the potato. And there it is, infiltrating the vehicle of the law. Similarly, at the end, the bicycle itself 'ticks' like a bomb into an uncertain future. And so Heaney builds into an ordinary enough childhood incident and the simple operations of the law a symbolic confrontation between repression and its representatives on the one hand and on the other, the dwellers on the land, indigenous as roots, storing themselves against the hour.

And yet, born to this atmosphere, Heaney's mind runs continually on the imagination and its works, on writers and artists, 'the singing school' of his overall title for the sequence. He names the writers with something approaching profligacy: Wordsworth, Yeats, Patrick Kavanagh, Joyce, Lorca, Katherine Mansfield, Hopkins are all mentioned in Part II of *North*. And there are two dedications to writers, Seamus Deane and Michael McLaverty. Read 'The Ministry of Fear' (pp. 129–31) and 'Fosterage' (p. 134) and you'll find some of the names. What do you see as the effect of all this naming? And read 'Exposure' (pp. 135–36). That too, bears on the question.

DISCUSSION

It's possible to see this listing as arch and self-conscious. But it would be a bit frowsty if we did. There are a number of useful things Heaney achieves by his literary list. First he makes the abstract sense we have of 'reading' and 'influence' concrete and present to us. In 'The Ministry of Fear' the young Heaney and Deane inhabit a world where they feel the contents of a book as immediately as the leather strap or the floodlights of the dogtrack, a world of endeavour and obsession where verses 'become a life'. This is autobiographical certainly, charting a friendship but, more widely, it contributes to a literary genre where the literary or artistic world presents itself as subject. Joyce's *Portrait of the Artist as a Young Man* is, in its university chapters, a good example. Some of Yeats's poems, like 'The Municipal Gallery Revisited', do a similar sort of thing. More widely Pope's *Dunciad* and, more narrowly, because more exclusively concentrated on the growth of a single mind, Wordsworth's *The Prelude* would help delineate such a genre. In other words, I'm suggesting that Heaney is not simply writing himself but constructing an image of a society. McLaverty's advice to him in 'Fosterage', Deane sending him 'bulky envelopes' and 'slim volumes', even his friends 'prismatic counselling' and Heaney weighing the destination and purpose of his 'responsible *tristia* . . . For the ear? For the people? For what is said behind-backs?', all is contributing to a society, the massively aroused world of Northern Irish and Irish writing in our time. Notice how the writers Heaney mentions are given life by making them seem to speak, or to be present to us, 'as Kavanagh said', 'Remember Katherine Mansfield' – 'that note of exile', 'Poor Hopkins'. All figure in a present world. At the same time the question these mentors in his 'Singing School' raise is the overwhelming one that faces Heaney and his writing, how art behaves in a time of political necessity. Wordsworth's *The Prelude* is quoted in one epigraph to 'Singing School', saying how he 'grew up / Fostered alike by beauty and by fear'.[17] In our preoccupation with Wordsworthian Nature we can easily forget how much of *The Prelude* and so how much of the growth of his mind and life was conditioned by the French Revolution. Yeats in the other epigraph first gets 'the pleasure of rhyme' from a 'book of Orange rhymes' and as a child thinks that he 'would like to die fighting the Fenians'. That intertwining of beauty and fear, art and violence, continues through the whole sequence, most of all in 'The Ministry of Fear', 'Summer

1969' and 'Exposure'. The final thing we might take from all these names is the presence of so many Irish ones. Indeed viewed exactly, and taking Hopkins as Welsh, there is only one English writer there. There are other traditions in play.

Another feature of these final poems is their colloquial style. The speaking manner of 'The Ministry of Fear', for example, is comparatively unusual in Heaney's writing up to this point. If this is an extension of his range of expression, what possibilities would you see in such a manner? Here I'm inviting you not only to indicate what 'The Ministry of Fear' achieves in itself but to think about – speculate – where it might lead? We wouldn't have to be right here; only to think about the uses of language.

DISCUSSION

Now to the colloquial tone. Especially in 'The Ministry of Fear' Heaney is using a very flexible manner, the lines approximating to the pentameter, ten syllables, and allowing varieties of conversation and idiom to take natural parts in the verse texture. So the allusions 'we have lived in important places', 'Here two on's are sophisticated' and the various voices, 'Catholics, in general, . . .', 'what's your name, Heaney?', 'What's your name, driver?' all fit more or less seamlessly into the overall flow. It is a verse speaking in tongues, not a tower of Babel. Such syntactic and rhythmic gear-changing is a profound ability in a poet. The apparent unforcedness and ease may make it difficult for us to see how good the writing is when we compare it with the more single-minded texture of, say, 'Funeral Rites', but its achievement is just as difficult. It's the sort of skill that can be learnt from Wordsworth's *The Prelude* or from Chaucer and is all to do with flexibility and variation deviating from but maintaining permanence and flow. Poetry is a lot to do with this mixture of 'information' and voice and the possibilities of such mixing are endless because it really stems from the poet's confidence to do many things and make them count and not just do the one thing well. If the fox has many tricks, the hedgehog one big one, then 'The Ministry of Fear' is Heaney as fox. 'Station Island' will be the more possible with it written.

One final thing. Applying the discussion of 'A Constable Calls' to 'The Ministry of Fear', the maximum degree of mixing, logically, is in the conjunction of opposites. So the implied content of 'What's your name, Heaney? . . .' and 'What's your name, driver? . . .' and the intonation of Seamus . . .' and '*Seamus?*', varying between enquiry and threat, between joke and fear, between culture and culture indeed, indicate, in each case, in virtually the same words, the deepest oppositions. It is back to Wordsworth's conjunction of opposites 'beauty' and 'fear'. I wonder how deliberately chosen Heaney's title is? There is, one suspects, an Orwellian tone to 'The Ministry of Fear', but contemporary with the chilling inventions of *1984*, it was the title of a novel by Graham Greene.[18] There it initially means a government department which operates through fear.

> It isn't only that they get a hold on certain people. It's the general atmosphere they spread, so that you feel you can't depend on a soul.[19]

But by the end of the book

> it wasn't the small Ministry to which Johns had referred, with limited aims like winning a war or changing a constitution. It was a Ministry as large as life to which all who loved belonged. If one loved one feared. That was something Digby had forgotten, full of hope among the flowers and *Tatlers*.[20]

and in the personal relationship that is the centre of the book:

> They had to tread carefully for a lifetime, never speaking without thinking twice; they must watch each other like enemies because they loved each other so much.

Fear and love are so mixed in Greene's book that they cannot unravel without destroying the love. In this way fear is 'ministry' in the sense of 'ministering' to the deepest, most loving ends. Does Heaney's sense of the North equally involve these commingling extremes, the utmost love, an exhausted fear?

North, to put it oversimply, is a book of two manners. In Part I material from history, myth, a contemplated geography is treated in short, highly finished lines. There is a slightly cryptic tone to it, often a sense of artefact. In Part II the line is longer, more colloquial, the materials drawn much more from the present and indeed from the political present. It is raw, its ear to the drumming ground. These two halves, I would suggest, are not dissonant but, like the white and the yolk of an egg, make one. In some sense each enables the other to exist by taking some of the burden of mixed expression from the poems, allowing a consistent tone to each. The range for instance, that Heaney achieves in 'Viking Dublin: Trial Pieces' (pp. 107–10) between

> These are trial pieces,
> The craft's mystery
> improvised on bone:
> foliage, bestiaries,
>
> interlacings elaborate
> as the netted routes
> of ancestry and trade
> (pp. 107–8)

and later in the sequence,

> 'Did you ever hear tell,'
> said Jimmy Farrell,
> 'of the skulls they have
> in the city of Dublin?'
> (p. 110)

is not easy to contain consistently in the one poem and it is a sensible strategy to hold the manners apart but let their implicit relationship emerge in the total setting of the book. I have already tried to suggest that the dedicatory poems 'Sunlight' and 'The Seed Cutters', by transfiguring the ordinary and the anonymous, give a frame for the mythic and the colloquial aspects of the book's savage materials. I want now to suggest that the final poem, 'Exposure' consummates the book. It is both the final poem of the sequence 'Singing School' and so a final act of 'fosterage' and the final poem of the book, the whole sequence called, in all its dimensions, *North*. Heaney is now living in Wicklow, south of the border, in the Republic, and he meditates on choices. Is this too a choice between manners, between a spent rhetoric and resignation to reality? Where in the poem would you see evidence for either? And is Wicklow a resting-place or an unquiet bed?

DISCUSSION

In a cold, unpromising, rain-sodden Wicklow, more a state of being than a landscape, Heaney, at the end of the year, among trees 'inheriting the last light', searches out portents, comets, falling stars, meteorites, and imagines a hero, committing his gift, presumably here, his poetry, to the defence of 'the desperate'. He imagines this because he is not, as he sees it, such a hero. But is it also that he is not convinced of the validity of the heroic posture? If he is not convinced of it, then, his chosen alternative, to weigh 'responsible *tristia*', may be, not defeat nor failure, but the better part. Nonetheless who would know? To whom, for whom does he speak? Heaney presents a somewhat Jacobean world, of gossip and information and malice – of betrayal 'behind-backs', 'let-downs', 'erosions'. From its extremes he has withdrawn, 'neither internee nor informer' and shrunk into exile, to a hermit-like contemplation, remote from the battle or, in his more telling word, the 'massacre'. Just as the domestic and personal world, in the dedicatory poems and in the poems of Part II, has here been transmuted into a Jacobean world, so now his poet's walk 'through damp leaves' also takes on mythic dimensions, in Tudor history, 'wood-kerne', and ecological ones, as he becomes identical with his environment 'Taking protective colouring / From bole and bark'. The two manners of the book, mythic and personal, coalesce. What is finally presented is not, I think, a myth of failure, and a confessional savouring of it, but rather a dedication to a possible scope. 'The once-in-a-lifetime portent' was not on the cards, but Heaney is still at the cutting edge of Northern life. He suffers exposure, does not merely come clean about where he stands. Politically alert it may be, but the mental struggle that goes on in this poem and, indeed, attends the whole of *North*, cannot be crudely politicized as a retreat from or an assent to one of two contending bigotries. There are certain irreducible positions that will obtain with a familial, sensitive, Catholic Nationalist from the North wherever he or she ends up. They are the mythic dimensions that sanction the personal life. They do not crudely prescribe political positions. Instead their ancestral weights and dignities will echo through and enrich the poems. As an accompaniment to these themes and perplexities, it would be good to read the first essay in Heaney's second collection of critical writings, 'The Interesting Case of Nero, Chekhov's Cognac and a Knocker', in *The Government of the Tongue* (1988).[22] This will also serve to anticipate some of the materials in my final two chapters.

5. *Field Work**

I suggested in my previous chapter that *North* was the most shaped of Heaney's books. 'The Grauballe Man' might be used to represent the mode of the whole book, its many angles of vision concentrated on a single subject, and used first to distance it, then to render it on a new plane. 'Singing School' shows how the matter of the North had developed and nurtured Heaney as an artist. And so the book overall

* *Selected Poems* gives out after *North* and so for this chapter and the final one I will, in as many instances as possible, print the poems for discussion. Some of the poems from *Field Work* (1979) are also available in *The Penguin Book of Contemporary British Poetry*[1] and, where that is the case, I'll refer you to it.

is to be seen as the proper outcome of the North's fosterage. Nonetheless the estimate Heaney gives of himself at the end of the book in 'Exposure' is not that of an artist who has come away with the spoils in a massive act of salvage, but of someone who has somewhere missed out. The book ends in County Wicklow, following Heaney's move South. He is withdrawn from the North in a resigned accommodation to the possible. *Field Work* (1975) goes on worrying away at the same set of questions and answers, which is natural enough, but attempts some other recourses to fill the void that comes with disengagement from the North. It might be felt that moving to the South is, for a man of Heaney's background, a return to the real home, but this is wrong. To see it as more completely home is in effect to deny the premise that could make it home at all. That premise is that the North is part of Ireland, in an extra-political sense, and so the South helps to bring its full reality to expression. But if that is the case the North must do the same for the South, and in Heaney's case, given the memories of childhood and community, it brings the reality to expression even more fully. In that sense a move to the South is an exile. 'An inner émigré' means that Heaney is exiled into his mind certainly but also that he is an exile in his own land. In Heaney's case it is politics and national boundaries that make him so, rather than temperament. Mostly he is not here out of sorts with the particular ranges of the Irish tradition that prompted Joyce into exile. The poems of *Field Work* are full of questions, so instead of me proposing the questions that we should ask, perhaps it would be right to follow up some of Heaney's own. In 'After a Killing' – 'Who's sorry for our trouble?'; in 'Sibyl', 'What will become of us?'; in 'The Badgers', 'How perilous is it to choose / not to love the life we're shown?'; in 'Glanmore Sonnets IX' – 'Did we come to the wilderness for this?' and 'What is my apology for poetry?'.

Let's begin with 'After a Killing', the first part of 'Triptych', three poems meditating the condition of Ireland. I will quote the whole poem for you.

After a Killing
There they were, as if our memory hatched them,
As if the unquiet founders walked again:
Two young men with rifles on the hill,
Profane and bracing as their instruments.

Who's sorry for our trouble?
Who dreamt that we might dwell among ourselves
In rain and scoured light and wind-dried stones?
Basalt, blood, water, headstones, leeches.

In that neuter original loneliness
From Brandon to Dunseverick

I think of small-eyed survivor flowers,
The pined-for, unmolested orchid.

I see a stone house by a pier.
Elbow room. Broad window light.
The heart lifts. You walk twenty yards
To the boats and buy mackerel.

And to-day a girl walks in home to us
Carrying a basket full of new potatoes,
Three tight green cabbages, and carrots
With the tops and mould still fresh on them.[2]

In the first stanza there are a number of words that direct the meaning strongly. Think about 'hatched', 'the unquiet founders', a reference to the guerrilla leaders who established the Irish Free State. Consider 'profane and bracing', 'instruments' and the effect of these words. In stanzas 2 and 3, Heaney seems to develop an image of isolation and loneliness. Is this a welcome or unwelcome state? Or just an inevitable one? And can we see stanzas 4 and 5 as offering some relief from the situation of the poem, which is, after all, after a killing? If we can, what gives relief?

DISCUSSION

'Hatched' is a loaded word. Its associations are not quite neutral. Among other possibilities, you can hatch chickens and you can hatch maggots. I think it is towards the disturbing possibilities of new birth that Heaney is directing us. Here though it is 'our memory' that does the hatching. The sight of the two men on the hill with their guns is less like something present to us now than a recollection of the 'unquiet founders'. What he sees is an echo, perhaps even a parody of the revolutionary founders of the modern Irish state, its independence achieved through guerrilla war. They are unquiet, presumably because Ireland is not yet unified and fully independent, but 'unquiet' and 'walked again' carry for most of us associations of restless, unplacated spirits who are themselves disturbing, even terrifying. Notice that Heaney adds to the hallucinatory sense, which mingles the 'young men' with the historical revolutionaries, by twice using 'as if'. This repetition also gives a meditative effect here, slowing, refining the thought, prayerlike, through repeating formulae. The modern gunmen would see themselves as spiritual and political descendants of the old Republican Army. Heaney's 'as if' reserves its judgement though. Maybe, maybe not. Perhaps it is only that men with guns inevitably remind us of other men with guns. Cause, time, place and effect may change. In this, 'instruments' is a well-chosen word. The gun itself is a mode of action, not good or bad in itself, its morality determined by its use. It is the instrument by which the young men act. And other instruments are conceivable. But if the direction of my wished-for reading is towards questioning the policies and modes of the young men, the phrase 'profane and bracing' reveals, not a divided mind in Heaney, but one capable of holding simultaneously, even if not synthesizing, different emotions about the revolutionaries' status. 'Profane' means something like 'defiling' but is used primarily as opposed to 'sacred'. At the same time it carries a sense of natural vigour. They and their rifles are 'profane' then, yet 'bracing'. There is an excitement, a tingle about the coupling of the words. Expressions like 'the resistance', 'freedom fighters' or 'rebels' work in the same way.

'Who's sorry for our trouble?' Heaney asks, and the answer this supposes is 'no one'. This may not be true, of course, but the effect of the question is to proclaim an isolation from sympathy, an isolation sustained from outside. The succeeding lines suggest a more fruitful isolation, dwelling 'among ourselves' in a world scoured to its basic properties, not wholly inviting, but in which it is possible to survive. Adam's neuter and lonely world before Eve is echoed on the face of Ireland and 'small-eyed' flowers survive. And so does the poet, given elbow room, broad light and a lifting heart by the unforced simplicities of life. Symbolic of that 'a girl walks in home to us' with carefully itemized vegetables, 'fresh', 'green' and 'new'. The ordinary sanctions a possible life.

Now I want you to read 'Casualty'.[3] You'll find a text handy in Blake Morrison's and Andrew Motion's *Penguin Book of Contemporary British Poetry* which includes a fair amount of Heaney and other Irish poets. Heaney incidentally wrote a poem 'An Open Letter' objecting to being included under the adjective 'British' in the title, for 'be advised / My passport's green', he says.[4] Interestingly 'Casualty' also has a revenant, not now one of the 'unquiet founders' but an ordinary fisherman. In the second stanza there is some by-play about poetry and Heaney avoiding talk about it. Again in stanza six, another of Heaney's qualities – his education – is brought into the poem. What role do you think Poetry and Education, as Heaney's particular attributes, have to play in the situation described in the poem? A brief comment on that situation. On Sunday 30 January 1972, soldiers of the First Battalion of the Parachute Regiment shot dead thirteen people during a civil rights march in the Bogside in Derry city. The fisherman who is the subject of the poem was blown up three days later when he broke an IRA curfew to go drinking.

DISCUSSION

It's important to see this poem as a kind of elegy, somewhat in the manner of Yeats's 'Easter 1916'. That poem too, posed questions, but its mood is triumphalist, even if it is triumph out of adversity. 'Casualty' is much more quizzical. First Heaney describes his friend's 'whole manner' in the bar. He has an environmental naturalness and ease, 'sidling tact' and a 'quick eye', and this extends through everything he does. When he tries to broach the subject of Heaney's 'other life', his poetry, Heaney, 'always politic', responds with the same covert skill so as to evade the question and 'switch the talk to eels' or whatever. Art, in the official sense, seems misplaced and awkward and yet the man's life is art and his life and death subject for it. Then Heaney briefly relates the fisherman's death in the aftermath of Bloody Sunday. He links it with the rest of the deaths as they cement the bonds of the Bogside and the common funeral 'braced and bound' them. It's easy enough, incidentally, to find out who the fisherman is and individualize him that way, but I don't want to do that. The anonymous 'he' that Heaney uses seems deliberate so that, while his specific qualities and character are clear to us, he seems to become generic for all the deaths of innocents in bars and on the streets, as anonymous and as specific as the score 'PARAS THIRTEEN . . . BOGSIDE NIL'. And where innocence is, what, indeed, is guilt? Heaney asks the question, not as to the guilt of bombers or soldiers but of the dead man himself.

> How culpable was he
> That last night when he broke
> Our tribe's complicity?

The guilt, if it is there, is to break the IRA curfew to drink 'in the gregarious smoke' and so break rank with his own people. But even as the question is asked, the dead man turns its imponderability back on the poet.

> 'Now you're supposed to be
> An educated man',
> I hear him say. 'Puzzle me
> The right answer to that one.'

There is no answer given. Heaney then describes his funeral and the car engines merge imperceptibly with the engine of the man's fishing boat in which Heaney had 'tasted freedom with him'. He imagines him returned to his

> proper haunt
> Somewhere, well out, beyond . . .

and asks him 'to question me again'. The dead question the lives of the living and Heaney invites those questions as necessary self-examination. In another poem, 'A Postcard from North Antrim', another dead man, Sean Armstrong, 'social worker of the town' is described as 'prince of no-man's land', but at the end of the poem is remembered 'chorus-leading, splashing out the wine'. Armstrong and the fisherman are outsiders who nonetheless, and perhaps because they are, express the best in their communities. As such they are models for the artist. But within the poem 'Casualty', Heaney, in his role as artist and educated man, is silent, evasive and nonplussed. The outsider here constructs himself not out of romantic vision but from ordinary living. He is not seeking 'the once-in-a-lifetime portent' but simple satisfaction from the ordinary. And that is the model for art that is growing in *Field Work*.

It grows a little more in the poem 'Song', here quoted entire.

Song
A rowan like a lipsticked girl.
Between the by-road and the main road
Alder trees at a wet and dripping distance
Stand off among the rushes.

There are the mud-flowers of dialect
And the immortelles of perfect pitch
And that moment when the bird sings very close
To the music of what happens.[5]

Clearly there is a very careful relationship between the two stanzas of this poem. What is it? And in what way is the rowan tree developed by Heaney's comments in the second stanza? An 'immortelle' is a type of flower which retains its colour when dried. It's more commonly, if less strikingly, called an everlasting flower.

DISCUSSION

The rowan has very bright orange-red berries, which in certain dull late-autumn lights seem almost luminous. That is how it's seen here, set against a background of alders 'at a wet and dripping distance'. And the location, as well as the background, is nondescript, 'between the by-road and the mainroad', neither here nor there. In these terms, it is an unlikely beauty, extravagant, even awkward, 'like a lipsticked girl', where the short i's and the clutches of consonants jerk the speech, nothing 'svelte' about the diction here. The girl of the image is unsophisticated, even gauche but beautiful, stepping transfigured from the drab background, and yet unquestionably part of it, not as foil only, but as dwelling. It is beauty perceived in the ordinary. The second stanza extends this sense of an absolute beauty in the ordinary through a series of parallels, beauties in dialectal speech, the gift of perfect pitch and finally birdsong, which, thought of as unconsidered art, has characteristically intrigued poets. He nets the whole sequence together very skilfully by linking the images of flowers and sound and moving from there to music; 'mud-flowers', 'dialect', 'immortelles', 'perfect pitch', 'sings', 'music'. I can't find the word 'mud-flowers' in a dictionary and am supposing it to be an invention of Heaney's, its sense indicated by the image in 'Gifts of Rain' (from *Wintering Out: Selected Poems*, p. 63).

> A man wading lost fields
> breaks the pane of flood:
>
> a flower of mud-
> water blooms up to his reflection
>
> like a cut swaying
> its red spoors through a basin.

There is, then, another movement happening here, between the momentary and the everlasting, between the detail and the pattern. The mud-flowers are necessarily individual and transitory beauties. Dialect is the pattern we construct from such individual occurrences. Perfect pitch enables us to hit the note moment by moment and always. And the birdsong happens moment by moment, but sometimes is perceived as close 'to the music' – the extended quality in which these moments have their being – 'of what happens'. I take this to be something like 'the music of the spheres', 'the real', and also the world of the ordinary, the daily, perceived as the world of reality. So the rowan's berries, their abrupt and luminous appearance, are the sudden moments which eternalize and construct their sodden backgrounds and display, not just a casual and fetching meaning, but meaning itself – 'the music of what happens'.

The ordinary then, 'the mud-flowers of dialect', Heaney seems to say in 'Song', takes art close to its centre. 'The Harvest Bow'[6] is another poem where this idea gains further nuance. Here, the natural world, 'straw' is used as the material of a folk-art, plaiting corn, in this case, the harvest bow. As you read the poem, however, I want to direct you to dissonant notes in it, as much as to this knowledge of a source for art. Is there unease in the poem and, if so, where do you locate it?

DISCUSSION

The situation in the poem is that Heaney has a harvest bow which, at the end of the poem, he pins up on 'our deal dresser'. Using it as an aid to thought, even contemplation, he 'tells' it (like the beads of a rosary) and fingers it 'like braille' and reconstructs the circumstances of its making, its maker and the place where it has come from. The maker would seem to be Heaney's father. I'm not sure how necessary it is to the poem that it should be him and not simply some close acquaintance of an older generation. But in stanza 4, 'that original townland / Still tongue-tied in the straw tied by your hand' may bear something of the familial loss and gain, pressure and nurture which Heaney examines in 'Follower' (*Selected Poems*, pp. 18–19). But do notice that Heaney identifies his father in 'Follower'. Here he does not. And so the widening and generalizing of the relationship may well be deliberate. This is an older folk-art, handed down, 'implicated' with ancestral messages – which brings us to the opening of the poem and perhaps already the seeds of dissonance. Heaney's use of 'implicate' is exact here. Literally, and in its origins, the word means to twist or twine into. Figuratively – and that these days is the main way it is used – it means to involve someone in something, for example, a crime. Of course there is no sense of crime in his usage here because what is folded into the harvest bow is the man's 'mellowed silence'. Nonetheless the word inevitably gives the idea that something always lies beneath appearances, that surfaces do not tell all. Similarly the expression 'wheat that does not rust' suggests that other things do rust and deteriorate. 'As it tightens twist by twist' has an inexorable sense about it. We know it describes the movement of skill and art but it is also the language of menace. After these tensions the point of arrival is safe, at least, 'knowable'. And yet the skill and art are expended on a 'love-knot', certainly, but one that is 'throwaway' and 'of straw' and art given, in no high-sounding way, to the everyday. This leads Heaney to think of the other skills of the hands ageing until they work in their sleep. So too Heaney's fingers trace 'unsaid' meanings from the straw he feels. And looking at the bow he recalls his childhood or his young manhood and the bric-a-brac of its passing, 'evening', 'blue smoke' rising, 'old beds and ploughs in hedges', 'an auction notice on an outhouse wall', 'homesickness'. The final sadness as the old man swishes at the weeds with his stick beating 'out of time' and 'flushes/Nothing' is the beautifully delayed consummation of Heaney's sequence of memories. And there is an ambiguity, uneasy doubt in his return now to the harvest bow. Is all that original world tied up like so many tongues and so speaking in the straw? Or is it prevented from speaking, 'tongue-tied', by the old man's hand? Heaney resolves the doubt with a bold, maybe overbold assertion, '*the end of art is peace*' and yet the 'device' (dubious word) is 'frail'. Its fixture is frail too, 'pinned' and it is in shape like a snare, through which the corn spirit has slipped, though warming it still. The assertion of the motto is wished-for rather than known. It aches, as does the whole of this dense and moving poem, for a viable art which tells of peace, but it cannot lay claim to it. In a way it's a poem which knows too much for its own quiet. Unlike the harvest bow, the poem thinks too much to be 'knowable' and 'throwaway'. Heaney sees nonchalance in the plaited corn and its art. He can see it but cannot inwardly achieve it.

In *Field Work* there are a number of poems which seem to celebrate nonchalance. It is in 'In Memoriam Sean O'Riada'[7] where he describes the *sprezzatura* of the Irish conductor-composer Sean O'Riada, key figure in the re-establishment of the traditions of Irish music, conducting the Ulster Orchestra and 'herding them south'. O'Riada works lying in the bottom of a boat 'listening to the cuckoo'. All is spontaneous but exact, natural, the gannet 'smacking through scales'. Heaney too, an old damaged pike, wants 'to swim in touch with soft-mouthed life' in 'The Guttural Muse'.[8] I suppose all this could be read as a wish to recover radical innocence, and set in a romantic mould, a world of unhurt instinct and art. In 'The Singer's House' people 'used to believe that drowned souls lived in the seals' and would swim in to hear a singer, as he sang, standing 'in the mouth of a whitewashed turf-shed'. 'Raise it again, man', Heaney says. 'We still believe what we hear'.[9] Is this whistling in the dark, the dark of politics and a spoiled land? It would be easy enough, and may be right to say so. But the assertion is itself an act which leaves the land less spoilt, expressing its truer identity. Music at least becomes, in a number of these poems, a measure and purveyor of actual life and we 'test the grieving registers for joy' as in 'September Song'.[10]

None of this is easy. It is made the more difficult in that the recourses that Heaney chooses to develop in his disengagement from the North are strongly private ones, art and the home. Art clearly, although privately conceived, has public ends and public needs. Above all, it needs – or, at least, relishes – an audience. It fixes its attention on public issues. But where the artist concentrates, as it were, on the means of production, on the creating mind, as has been the custom since the Romantics, it is inevitably private. Who really wants to know about the artist's mind? Other artists? No, by and large – they're already far too preoccupied with their own. Critics? Well, probably, but this is not too sustaining to the artist, who is all too prone to bite the hand that feeds on him. Psychologists? Some perhaps, but rats are more amenable than poets to preordained testing. And in any case who really wants to be a case-history, even in a catalogue of genius? Mostly what we want from poets is poems, not poems about poems. And so, underlying Heaney's generous ranging around the dimensions of a possible art, is a problematic concern, which, in its raw state, will not quite translate into poems. You can ponder the state of your art too much.

Involved in all art is a transmutation. In it, the life we perceive is subsumed in style, in form and measure. Sometimes, indeed, the art can cease to honour the life it issues from and cut the artist off from that sustaining life. It is this problem, part of the same range of concerns I have been inviting you to examine in these poems from *Field Work*, that seems to surface in 'The Badgers'; how do we relate to the life that is around us, the life we are presented with? Here is the poem.

The Badgers
When the badger glimmered away
into another garden
you stood, half-lit with whiskey,
sensing you had disturbed
some soft returning.

The murdered dead,
you thought.
But could it not have been
some violent shattered boy
nosing out what got mislaid
between the cradle and the explosion,
evenings when windows stood open
and the compost smoked down the backs?

Visitations are taken for signs.
At a second house I listened
for duntings under the laurels
and heard intimations whispered
about being vaguely honoured.

And to read even by carcasses
the badgers have come back.
One that grew notorious
lay untouched in the roadside.
Last night one had me braking
but more in fear than in honour.

Cool from the sett and redolent
of his runs under the night,
the bogey of fern country
broke cover in me
for what he is:
pig family
and not at all what he's painted.

How perilous is it to choose
not to love the life we're shown?
His sturdy dirty body
and interloping grovel.

> The intelligence in his bone.
> The unquestionable houseboy's shoulders
> that could have been my own.[11]

What attitudes to the badgers are taken in the poem? And what do the badgers represent in the final stanza? What is the particular force of the word 'choose' in that stanza?

DISCUSSION

I detect a number of attitudes. First the badgers are presented as mysterious, unlooked for, simply occurring in our world without our volition. They are figures for the mysteriousness of other lives. All this is there in the first stanza, in 'glimmered away' and in the sense of disturbing 'some soft returning'. The effect of being 'half-lit with whiskey' is not just to add a bit of local colour, but to add a further level of mysteriousness to the encounter, an imprecision in the observer's own faculties. Then taking off from there, the imagination suggests possibilities, 'the murdered dead' or some revenant 'shattered boy'. These are ghostly presences and seem like portents – 'Visitations are taken for signs' echoing Eliot's line in 'Gerontion', 'Signs are taken for wonders'.[12] But now the badgers' visits are seen as bestowing on us some kind of vague honour. In the fourth stanza one becomes an object of fear. And then 'the bogey of the fern country' is revealed as 'pig family'. This is presented as an accurate view as distinguished from the mysterious, romantic and emotionally heightened views presented earlier. Heaney then asks his decisive question

> How perilous is it to choose
> not to love the life we're shown?

What dangers are there in rejecting the life we are presented with? In the case of the badgers Heaney sees them as an apt symbol for himself.

> The intelligence in his bone.
> The unquestionable houseboy's shoulders
> that could have been my own.

To reject the badgers as they are, in favour of the falsifying views earlier in the poem, would be to reject himself and what he has come from. We can choose not to love what is given to us, reject what we are. Such rejection is not thrust upon us from outside. The choice is implicit in our decisions. And it may be endangering if we back off from the realities, divert them, even into the ways of art. Poetry of all arts, perhaps, cannot shrug off its interplay with the world of action.

Heaney's poems do not. But if that is so, art for him cannot be a recourse in retreat from the world. It can instead recognize more profoundly other amplitudes from the world. To come full circle in this series of discussions, it will see and celebrate the badgers for what they are; and the 'whole manner' of the fisherman in 'Casualty'; 'the mud-flowers of dialect'; the gift that makes no more than 'a throwaway love-knot of straw'; the girl bringing fresh vegetables 'in home to us' 'after a killing'. If art is to be read as escape then an art of this kind, salve though it may be, will serve to embed Heaney deep in his milieu, a consummation he ultimately wishes for. He is not in retreat in Wicklow or elsewhere. At the most it is a strategic withdrawal, to regroup.

Domesticity and its poetry might remain as escape 'from the massacre' but it is only by remaining private that it can be a genuine escape. Once it is poetry, it is public and one's private life is up for critical grabs. This is a dilemma. How does a writer celebrate the private gain of home without infringing its privacy? Such a dilemma does not have to be expressed to exist, a shadow over the writing, making the tone insecure, where security is all. For example, Heaney has a witty poem 'An Afterwards' about the egotistical demands or impositions of the writing life. In the midst of all its Dantesque comedy the writer's wife says

> 'Why could you not have, oftener, in our years
> Unclenched, and come down laughing from your room
> And walked a twilight with me and your children –
> Like that one evening of elder bloom
> And hay, when the wild roses were fading?'[13]

and these lines with their directness and unmodified romanticism make the wit that preoccupies the other twenty lines of the poem gratuitous and tawdry. Of course it is not Heaney alone, or mainly, who finds trouble here. Heaney has avoided the excesses of so-called confessional poetry, but has, at least sometimes, fallen into the trap of a too-shaping formalism. On the one hand, confession implies a self-revelation so frank and absolute as to be at odds with the formal shapes and restraints of art. On the other, if the forms and manners achieve the distance the poem requires, they may abolish the closeness and contact that the human situation asks.

The problem here is that poets are constantly enjoined to write of what they know; and by and large what we all now know is some degree or other of home and garden. So the area of reserve, comfort and quietude is forced out into the open, as public subject. Once poetic subjects were the great affairs of state or revealed spiritual truths, and here private anguishes could coincide exactly with public feeling. But public rhetoric jostles awkwardly with the more closeted intimacies of marriage. There are possible rhetorics here – or close by – and one I think that can work well is the rhetoric of friendship. The poetry of friendship has a long history and takes something like a modern form in Coleridge's 'This Lime Tree Bower my Prison'.[14] Yeats in 'In Memory of Major Robert Gregory'[15] is working similar ground and Heaney often uses this range well in *Field Work*, not as his sole subject in any given poem but as contributing to a total effect. This he does in 'September Song', 'A Postcard from North Antrim' and a little as background in 'Elegy'[16], a fine tribute to a poet who has moved sometimes consummately, sometimes uneasily through the ranges of poeticized domesticity, Robert Lowell. In 'Elegy', Heaney recognizes the difficulties such writing exemplifies, and speaks of Lowell's 'whole craft', its

> course set wilfully across
> the ungovernable and dangerous.

'Wilfully' is a very carefully placed word. Lowell's choices are deliberate, perhaps culpable. His magisterial presence also illuminates another aspect of the domestic, that the roles of the married – husband, wife and parenthood – do not automatically annul the hungers of childhood still within one.

> You found the child in me
> when you took farewells
> under the full bay tree
> by the gate in Glanmore,
>
> opulent and restorative
> as that lingering summertime,
> the fish-dart of your eyes
> risking, 'I'll pray for you.'

There is another intertwining here then, that could relieve the singular pressures of domestic poetry, when the familial pattern becomes an image echoing other wider structures. Lowell becomes enmeshed in Heaney's array of ancestors, American poet lining up with Irish farmer, artist alongside artisan. 'I'll pray for you', in Lowell's jokey seriousness, is a post-Catholic quip, recognized by both men as intentional and meant. So the domestic moment, conviviality with American friend and poet, immediate prelude to Lowell's death by heart attack, is raised to elegy and becomes itself part of art's

> deliberate, peremptory
> love and arrogance.

This brings us to 'Glanmore Sonnets', a sequence of ten sonnets, four of which are printed in the *Penguin Book of Contemporary*

British Poetry. I will give numbered references to the sonnets in my account. By now we have become used to Heaney's sequences which, although not precisely narrative, do have beginnings, middles and ends. But the sonnets, partly because they are sonnets, prone to the statuesque and thick-textured, seem to be, each one, complete and mainly to relate by aggregation. There is sequence, but it sets up a state rather than an ending. Heaney constantly assumes interim positions as if waiting for something. In the early books this took the form of offering poetic manifestos which would be, in time, complete. Here though, no position is proclaimed. In so far as a position is meant to emerge it is interim and known to be so. Glanmore, Heaney's new home in Wicklow, is a respite, a resting place for the escaping lovers, figured in two such pairs, Lorenzo and Jessica, and Dairmuid and Grainne (Sonnet X). But Heaney brings with him the whole equipage of the past, the ground opened and deeply tilled. He is

> quickened with a redolence
> of the fundamental dark unblown rose. (I)

This is the Roisin Dubh, Dark Rosaleen, the lover symbol which is Ireland, and his ghosts come striding, sowing their dream Easter grain. Glanmore is a hedge-school for him (II). The hedge-schools were the makeshift schools by which the rural Irish kept the semblance – and often more than the semblance – of education going through the penal times. The tip of a manifesto shows here. Heaney hopes to raise a voice 'that might continue, hold, dispel, appease' and to nurture it, comes to 'this strange loneliness' (III). Various memories succeed, some augmented by the present sights and sounds, the boortree – the elderberry, beautifully described and his childhood tree house, 'where small buds shoot and flourish' (V), and the ripples on the drinking water set off by shunting engines on the railway (IV). There is a trepidation, a shaking of the heart in this image which is repeated again in Sonnet VIII when a succession of imagined and remembered horrors or poignancies force from him the cry 'Come to me quick, I am upstairs shaking'. 'Did we come to the wilderness for this?' he asks when his old horror, a rat, balances on a briar outside the window (IX). And this prompts the further question 'What is my apology for poetry?' But the respite of the final sonnet is anticipated even among these tremblings from a pursuing past. Heaney, perhaps objectifying himself in the third person, sees himself, in an image of daring, as striving for even fuller insights:

> 'I will break through', he said, 'what I glazed over
> With perfect mist and peaceful absences . . .' (VI)

and Glanmore, or more accurately the sea-roads off the Wicklow coast, 'marvellous and actual' are a 'haven' (VII). The compound in the sonnets, the state they establish, is not of quietude, nor fully resolved. The North is not escaped because the powerful conditions of our lives cannot be escaped. They can be alleviated but not eliminated. *Field Work* as a whole, and epitomized in these highly condensed sonnets, is still an unquiet book because it is too soon to take rest, except in dream, and even then 'exposed all night in a wetting drizzle'. Respite, if not escape, is possible and

> Outside a rustling and twig-combing breeze
> Refreshes and relents. Is cadences. (III)

Heaney's dominant recourses in *Field Work* are domesticity and art. Neither is new. But they are used in a new way. The domestic world had hitherto been primarily something given and set in the geography of childhood. In 'Mossbawn' the 'space' is to be located in a childhood kitchen. Now, in the move South, both home and geography have to be newly created. That is to say we are no longer concerned to seek in the past a ground for action but to see creating that ground as action itself. The pressure is less, then, to the meditative role, the long-haired and thoughtful 'wood-kerne/ Escaped from the massacre' of 'Exposure', regretting the 'diamond absolutes', than to the active role, seeking in ordinary and proximate things an abolute. This impulse, away from the meditative, I think one can say, is a reaction against Heaney's habitual temperament. In the opening poem in *Field Work* 'Oysters',[17] he eats oysters, and though enjoying them and the occasion, nonetheless sees them as 'alive and violated', 'ripped', 'shucked' and 'scattered'. Then, in a flashback, which, in the ordinary way of things, is scarcely implied in his own present meal, he sees the Romans hauling their oysters across the Alps, to Rome, where they are eaten, glutting 'privilege'. This habit of thinking too much, of seeing too deep into things, angers him

> that my trust could not repose
> In the clear light, like poetry or freedom
> Leaning in from sea.

It is a rebellion against paralysis through thought. 'Poetry' and 'freedom' are romantic properties maybe but they are, for Heaney, key desires and seem not to be possible if the habits of thought and counter-thought prevent action. Interestingly this series of alignments makes poetry active rather than sedentary. It is therefore entirely right that Heaney's wish for action should be expressed in terms of a linguistic analogy at the end of the poem, that he might become 'verb, pure verb'. Heaney wants no modifiers, no parenthesis, only verb. Thinking too much is not only temperamental though. It is a product of having too much to think about. The predicates of Heaney's North-South, active-passive make-up can present themselves as rich in possibility or as paralysing. Near the close of *Field Work* there is a moving tribute to a too-little-known Irish poet, Francis Ledwidge.[18] He was an Irish nationalist who died at Ypres in 1917, fighting, like many other Irishmen, in the British army. The poem very skilfully intercuts childhood memories of a First World War memorial at Portstewart with incidents from Ledwidge's life in Ireland, in the Dardanelles and on the Western Front, along with quotations from Ledwidge's own writings – 'to be called a British soldier while my country / Has no place among nations'. And then Heaney makes all this intercutting into the meaning of the poem. Ledwidge, confused as to allegiance, or rather loyal to two allegiances, in love and rejected in love, an Irish poetic ruralist forgotten in the trenches of British war poetry, is now dead like the unambiguous 'true-blue ones' named on the Portstewart memorial. 'All of you consort now underground' who followed 'the sure confusing drum'. Heaney uses the word 'our' which often signals his laying claim to continuities with a past.

> In you, our dead enigma, all the strains
> Criss-cross in useless equilibrium.

Ledwidge is the enigma which is the unresolved condition of Ireland, and Heaney sees himself as part of that 'useless equilibrium' hearing once more 'the sure confusing drum'.

The way out of this is Heaney's 'pure verb' of 'Oysters', but it isn't into the sensational world of armed men on the hills. Rather he thinks of simple existences. It is, if you like, the beginnings of domesticity. This is not written in order to align Heaney with a rural past which guarantees him continuous relationship with his ancestry and so gives Ireland its meaning. Rather it guarantees a possible present, a salve against 'our trouble', the succession of atrocious deaths. It gives 'elbow room'. In 'Sibyl', second part of 'Triptych', Heaney asks the prophetess 'What will become of us?' As part of her reply she says 'My people think money / And talk weather'.[19]

Ireland has habitually been sustained by ideal visions of itself in which economic considerations have been a means to an end, never ends in themselves. But the new Ireland which Heaney encounters in the South is getting to be a little like everywhere else in its priorities. For the Heaney-inspired Sibyl this adds to the 'comfortless noises' of 'our island'. It perhaps shows how much Heaney accepts the reality of the visions that had propelled the early makers of the Republic. Ireland as a land of milk and money is less attractive. But the ideal is nothing grandiose. It is, in the words of the American poet Adrienne

Rich, 'difficult ordinary happiness'.[20] Viewed only slightly more grandiosely it is something like the art of living. *Field Work* is an attempt to construct the terms possible to such an art in a world beleaguered by guns and money. As he suggests in the first of the Glanmore Sonnets,

> Now the good life could be to cross a field
> And art a paradigm of earth new from the lathe
> Of ploughs.

6. *Station Island* and After

I want in this chapter to give some account of Heaney's three most recent books *Sweeney Astray* (1983), *Station Island* (1984) and *The Haw Lantern* (1987). The summary nature of such an account will allow me to draw together some of the strands in the earlier part of this book and also to attempt an overview of Heaney to date. I want also, however briefly, to look at Heaney as a critic. I have used *Preoccupations* (1984) at various points in my account up to now. Here I will draw my examples from *The Government of the Tongue* (1988). In all this the high point for me – because of what it attempts – is the long sequence 'Station Island', so I will concentrate on that.

First, to restate and summarize my particular critical method. Throughout these discussions I have supposed that the poetic text can be read as a system of relationships between its various terms. I have tended to concentrate on the words, seen as elements of content or 'information', on oppositional relationships in meaning, in types of language, syntactical pattern and so on, and on the intersection of opposed 'verbal registers' or vocabularies. This I have done, not because these are the only possible sets that need to be examined but because they seem to me the most fruitful. It has been my point that these various oppositions are held in balance by the overall structure of the poem they generate and that it is precisely the point of poems to achieve such balances, not so much to resolve them as to keep them in play, to snatch ordered but not static sets from randomness. They are lifelike not primarily because they imitate the palpable conditions of life – that is an added extra – but because they provide clarifying models of experience. It is clear that myths, for example, are powerful structures which are assumed to do this. They are recurring patterns in the mind and in societies to which everyday experience can be related and by which it can be evaluated. At the same time I have remained conscious that any pattern that is derived within a poem can only be meaningful if it is not seen as simply self-referential. It occurs in human situations. And if discovering schemes of relationship allows us to describe the poem, by that same token we must place the poems in other schemes of relationship outside themselves. The poet will find some of those outside relationships confirmatory and releasing; others problematic and inhibiting. The poetry is always at the centre of contending forces. In this, Heaney is both typical and, because of the strength of the Northern pressures, exemplary. The constraints that have been operating on *Field Work*, to take our last subject, are not, I believe, to be found largely in the choice of subjects that Heaney feels called upon to make but lie rather in how those subjects may properly act within the poetry. How direct or how circumspect can he be? And again this is not so much a question of how fully he volunteers his autobiography to us but of what is right for the poetry? In that sense we should not be looking for self-revelation or to be able to say Heaney feels this or that. What the poem needs to be is a cutting edge that lays open some aspect of the world's condition. In this the personality of the poet is instrument and not end. Poetry concerned with the poet's mental make-up or deeply personal situation tends to obscure this much as novels and soap-operas are always getting confused with life. There is too much of the slice of life and too little of the clarified pattern that is the shaped key to the randomness of experience. So Heaney's question is always, how do we respond poetically to what happens to us and to what, in life, we make happen? How do we shape, not experience but our responses to experience? This implies always a certain uneasiness when the requirements of realism impose themselves on poets too strongly. Realism is the most deceiving of all artistic codes because it can look as if it is no code at all.

This need to externalize in order to make intelligible is the strong driving force in *Station Island*.[1] Put another way, Heaney is seeking new myths, new exemplary materials that can act as a repeating and containing model for experience, and not simply be contained by or adumbrate experience. In *North*, Viking history and archaeological remains acted as such a myth and delivered up meanings which were at once, impersonal, in so far as Heaney was not himself a Viking, universal in so far as they concerned notions like sacrifice and the simultaneous occurrence of death and joy, and local in so far as they provided a pattern of meaning for the doorstep horrors of the North of Ireland. This local aspect is important because it provides the point of contact between the writer and the chosen myth, just as clouds, bigger than counties, fall locally as rain.

Claude Lévi-Strauss tells a story about a peasant woman who goes to church while visiting another village and is the only one not to laugh at a joke in the priest's sermon. Asked why she didn't laugh, she said, 'I don't belong to the parish'. Lévi-Strauss goes on, 'In all language phenomena, there is more than just communication: there is also an attempt to work out modes of communication which are peculiar to a particular group, or generation, or social environment'.[2] It is doubt about what his locale, 'his parish' is that forces Heaney towards new myths. And he needs them, as most artists do, to avoid the very modern danger of becoming a locale of one.

As myth, Glanmore had not had quite enough force. It is respite and in that sense therapeutic rather than energizing. It doesn't break the mould. Nor does *Station Island* immediately. The poems in Part I seem often to traverse old ground and excite more because they are well done than because they explore. The poems are like so many dogs running in the same colours and bursting from the same traps.

The feeling is of random objects stirring memories and pointing morals, swept together, never quite acquiring collective shape, 'somewhere between / balance and inanition'.[3] It would not be silly to see this as occurring precisely because that is what Heaney intends them to be, a drawing together and using up of the themes and manners of a past, an act of clearance. He sees himself in 'Sandstone Keepsake' as 'a silhouette not worth bothering about', 'one of the venerators' rather than as true sacrificed victim, martyr, saint or villain.[4] The poems are sparring immaculately for openings. Three poems in particular seem to suggest where an opening might occur. 'Chekhov on Sakhalin' dramatizes an episode from Chekhov's life when his friends give him a bottle of cognac before he visits the island prison of Sakhalin in Tsarist Russia to interview the convicts. When he has drunk the bottle he smashes it on the stones

> In the months to come
> It rang on like the burden of his freedom
> To try for the right tone – not tract, not thesis –
> And walk away from floggings.[5]

and the attempt to 'waken the free man' in himself is not easy. Heaney is interested in this episode because it parallels his own dilemmas with regard to the North. How to escape and get the right tone while haunted by the ringing chains and implicated with them? But this is not self-dramatization. It is story-telling. Heaney lends his experience to give expression to Chekhov rather than coerces Chekhov to his own needs. Again in 'A Migration' he tells quite simply the story of the harrowing but ordinary migration of an Irish family returning from Glasgow to Wicklow, missing their connection and walking south through the night from Dublin. One of the daughters, Brigid, is Heaney's point of concentration for the poem and when, with them all at a low ebb,

> . . . the first drops of rain
> spit in the dark, Brigid
> gets up and says, 'Come on'.[6]

it is as if he assimilates but does not commandeer the girl's dogged courage. Again the realization is like a dramatist's when the poet uses what Eliot called the 'third voice' of poetry, when a character speaks in character and not as mouthpiece.[7] Finally, the last poem in the section 'The King of the Ditchbacks'[8] is a dramatization of the seventh-century Irish King Sweeney who was, in Flann O'Brien's words, turned into 'a bloody bird' and leapt from tree to tree the length and breadth of Ireland.[9] Sweeney will be the subject of the final section of the book, 'Sweeney Redivivus' (Sweeney revived or resurrected) and of Heaney's translation of the early Irish poem *Buile Suibhne*. Heaney's version *Sweeney Astray* appeared in 1983 in Ireland and in 1984 with Faber. 'The King of the Ditchbacks' is carefully placed, I think, to highlight the final section of the book. 'Station Island', the second section, is a considerable achievement. And it is also something of a watershed, but the first outflow of its waters is 'Sweeney Redivivus'. I have called 'King of the Ditchbacks' a dramatization of Sweeney but it is not quite that. It is about Heaney's own sense of coalescing with Sweeney while he is translating the Irish poem and his perception of an *alter ego*, at times an identity, not so much shadow as his own substance. I call it dramatization because, again, its direction is very firmly towards an understanding of a character other than Heaney himself. The self-examination is possible only because Sweeney is established in his own terms. The secret of this move from 'the growth of the poet's mind' is, of course, the act of translation that working on Sweeney has meant. Heaney says

> I was sure I knew him. The time I'd spent obsessively in that upstairs room bringing myself close to him: each entranced hiatus as I chain-

> smoked and stared out the dormer into the grassy hillside I was laying myself open. He was depending on me as I hung out on the limb of a translated phrase . . .[10]

If I can express what is happening simply and perhaps beyond the terms which are natural to it, Heaney is here giving before he receives. I speak of the poetic process only, not the human life, which we do not infer. Auden, in his curriculum for a College of Bards, suggests a number of things that the poets should do. One is to keep a little animal, another is to engage in a major act of translation.[11] And of course Lowell is another indicator here with his signal volume *Imitations* (1962). The importance of these things is that they are acts of free giving, measurable and contained. What you work to establish in translation, for example, is already the construct of another's mind. You, in Heaney's word, 'foster'. Until now – and it is the ancestral lookback – he has been fostered, and the things he has contemplated have also fostered him. Sweeney, the mad old Irish king, needs Heaney to project him into the current world. This is not to ignore Flann O'Brien's *At Swim-Two-Birds* where he is an important presence, but, in a way, to fulfil it. *At Swim-Two-Birds* will be, for most people, a more accessible book after Heaney's *Sweeney Astray*. The result of this fostering is, however, reciprocal. The effect of obsessively getting it right, so that Sweeney will live, is that 'my stealth was second nature to me, as if I were coming into my own', and later, – who is speaking, Sweeney or Heaney? –

> . . . my vision was a bird's
> at the heart of a thicket
>
> and I spoke as I moved
> like a voice from a shaking bush
>
> . . .
>
> And I saw myself
> rising to move in that dissimulation,
>
> top-knotted, masked in sheaves, noting
> the fall of birds: a rich young man
>
> leaving everything he had
> for a migrant solitude.

Heaney has one last necessary act to carry out before reviving himself with Sweeney. Like Eliot at the end of *The Waste Land* he will set his 'lands in order' and it will be by the same process, of converting a 'heap of broken images' to coherent form. If *North* is, so far, Heaney's most complete book, then arguably the sequence 'Station Island' is his most complete poem. Its setting is the pilgrimage site Station Island in Lough Derg, County Donegal. This is St Patrick's

Purgatory which, certainly since the early Middle Ages, has been an important centre of penitential pilgrimage. Its fame was once European but now its pull is probably felt only in Ireland. A number of writers including William Carleton, Denis Devlin, Patrick Kavanagh and Sean O'Faolain have set stories or poems within pilgrimages here and it does give the writer a number of peculiar advantages.[13] It establishes through privation and meditation, in a remote setting an atmosphere of self-examination and, often enough, spiritual resolve. So while solving many problems of narrative in this stationary, but recollective setting, it allows free movement of the mind. Crisis and insight are made simultaneously available, not to clear saints, but to the ordinary people of Ireland. Kavanagh's 1942 poem *Lough Derg* had concentrated on quasi-mystical insight within the ordinariness of life.

> The middle of the island looked like the memory
> of some village evicted by the Famine,
> Some corner of a field beside a well
> old stumps of walls where a stunted boortree is growing.
> These were the holy cells of saintly men –
> O that was the place where Mickey Fehan lived
> And the Reillys before they went to America in the Fifties.
> No, this is Lough Derg in county Donegal –
> So much alike is our historical
> And spiritual pattern, a heap
> of stones anywhere is consecrated
> By love's terrible need.[14]

Kavanagh's poem seems never to have been revised and, as it were, 'prepared' for publication. In the words of the contemporary Irish poet Paul Durcan, 'it exhales the white-hot power of a poem which was composed at one sitting'.[15] Heaney's 'Station Island' is not at all like that. It achieves its power through care, its insight through meditation rather than by thunderbolt. But Kavanagh is one of Heaney's 'fosterers' here, in Section V of the poem 'slack-shouldered and clear-eyed' although he doesn't say much, only maybe to remind Heaney of the continuities of Irish patterns and the preoccupations of artists in Ireland. 'Forty-two years on and you've got no farther!' 'But after that again, where else would you go?'(V) The place, Lough Derg, is an expressive and exploratory image, it is not too much to say, for a central strand of Irish writing. Designedly here, Heaney comes up against himself and his country, in Kavanagh's account, 'our historical and spiritual pattern'. Heaney's use of the location is as a point for him to meet with a succession of ghosts or recollections from an actual past, together with formative writers or advisers, Carleton, Kavanagh and, closing the whole sequence, James Joyce.

On the way he encounters the tinker 'old Sabbath-breaker', Simon Sweeney, who shouts after him 'Stay clear of all processions!' (I) He meets 'a young priest from his past', 'glossy as a blackbird', now ravaged, physically and spiritually from his work on the foreign missions. 'What are you doing,' he asks Heaney, 'Unless you are here taking the last look?' (IV) Religion emerges here, in a way different from its former appearances in Heaney's work. Up till now, it has presented itself in the main, as tribal definition, engrained so as to produce images for use in the mind and in the poems, but not as a central drive in the poems. Here it does present itself with that 'gravity'. I choose that word to throw discussion back to the poem 'Westering' which also has this seriousness attaching to it. And 'Limbo' and 'Bye-Child' close by in the same book, *Wintering Out*, seem drawn into the same circle. Later in 'Station Island', Section XI, jostling James Joyce for pole position, comes St John of the Cross, with the range of imagery that had figured in *Door into the Dark*. Is it image here or deeper intention? This other priest says

> 'Read poems as prayers . . . and for your penance
> translate me something by Juan de la Cruz.' (XI)

but he also says other things which, at the least, are good advice. He spoke

> about the need and chance
>
> to salvage everything, to re-envisage
> the zenith and glimpsed jewels of any gift
> mistakenly abased . . . (XI)

'He had made me feel' says Heaney 'there was nothing to confess' and he fulfils his penance in a majestic translation

> How well I know that fountain, filling, running,
> although it is the night. (XI)

and, in closure,

> I am repining for this living fountain.
> Within this bread of life I see it plain
> although it is the night. (XI)

It is not only the priest who tells him to salvage everything. William Carleton, the nineteenth-century rural Irish writer, as impatient as he was in 1829 in his *Lough Derg Pilgrim*, sees Heaney, on pilgrimage, and says

> 'O holy Jesus Christ, does nothing change?' (II)

Continuities are all the time, with Kavanagh, with Carleton and with the priest from the missions, being summoned up to be questioned.

But the questions, it must be remembered, are also questioned. Heaney and Carleton swap their backgrounds which have much in common. Carleton characterizes himself

> I who learned to read in the reek of flax
> and smelled hanged bodies rotting on their gibbets
> and saw their looped slime gleaming from the sacks –
>
> hard-mouthed Ribbonmen and Orange bigots
> made me into the old fork-tongued turncoat
> who mucked the byre of their politics. (II)

And Heaney, though not driven to these lengths for survival, recalls the elements in Carleton's stories which he too 'heard and did'

> flax-pullings, dances, summer crossroads chat . . .
> And always, Orange drums.
> And neighbours on the roads at night with guns. (II)

Carleton, in a line of recognition as strongly emphasized as Lear's repeating 'never',[17] says

> 'I know, I know, I know, I know', he said,
> 'but you have to try to make sense of what comes' (II)

and Heaney grasps at the objects of salvage, the unremarkable presences of life. I say 'unremarkable' because central to our view of what is of note is the presence or absence of a mental rhetoric which has to be controlled if we are not to falsify what we see and so, what we know. In part this is what the ghost of Colum McCartney accuses him of in Section VIII. McCartney was the subject of 'The Strand at Lough Beg' in *Field Work*. There Heaney, with reference to Dante's tall rushes growing from the oozy strand (in *Purgatorio* 1, 103), makes an elegy which ends

> I lift you under the arms and lay you flat.
> With rushes that shoot green again, I plait
> Green scapulars to wear over your shroud.

In Section VIII, Heaney accuses himself, through the figure of McCartney, of falsifying fact, concentrating on 'the strand empty at daybreak'

> 'You saw that, and you wrote that – not the fact.
> You confused evasion and artistic tact.
> The Protestant who shot me through the head
> I accuse directly, but indirectly, you
> who now atone perhaps upon this bed
> for the way you whitewashed ugliness and drew
> the lovely blinds of the *Purgatorio*
> and saccharined my death with moving dew.' (VIII)[16]

The questions are 'how to make sense of what comes', what tone to use and finally what questions to ask. James Joyce, in the last section of the poem is sharp with Heaney, telling him, roughly speaking, to get on with it.

> 'Your obligation
> is not discharged by any common rite
> . . . The main thing is to write
> for the joy of it . . .
> Let go, let fly, forget.
> You've listened long enough. Now strike your note'.

And in so far as this is specific to manner, but not to matter, he adds some negative hints, outlawing the concern about the Irish and the English languages 'Who cares any more?' he says. 'You are raking at dead fires'. And for good measure, adds

> 'That subject people stuff is a cod's game,
> infantile, like your peasant pilgrimage.' (XII)

His advice is to find 'signatures on your own frequency'. Now it has to be borne in mind that this is Joyce speaking and that Heaney, taking off from his handling of 'Chekhov at Sakhalin', 'A Migration', and 'The King of the Ditchbacks', has a strong sense of the characters he is presenting. And this we can infer would be Joyce's advice since it precisely follows his own development, a cutting loose from external pressures to respond only to the demands of art. Nonetheless, Heaney provides the words and directs them to his own condition and although there are many pieces of advice in the sequence, these are the words which send him on his way at the end of it. I would only try out one comment here. In Ireland, which is a country where passion means that constraints, whether of religion, politics or morality, or indeed of passion itself, are powerfully felt by individuals and powerfully presented and preserved by institutions, the least institutionalized and most individual area of the country's possibilities can often be portrayed as an escape from encircling prohibitions and manipulations. It will seem true to one's being where all else is less than true.

That area is art and the products of art. But this I suspect may be a false portrayal. Art does not operate outside a social context, nor without subjects. And it is not a subject of itself – at least not for artists, only for aestheticians. And Joyce, of course, is the proof of it. *Ulysses* and *Finnegan's Wake*, however much determined by the vocation of artist, are not cut off from the contexts of society, least of all of Irish society. Joyce – or Stephen Dedalus – was concerned to forge 'the uncreated conscience of the race' and was as coercive as the rest of the manipulators in that. So Heaney's withdrawal from these frays can only reasonably come with a sense of having paid, and more than paid his dues, to those questions, whether they're 'cod's game' or not. Art *per se* is as much a snare as anything. And judging by the way 'Sweeney Redivivus' works out – the first fruits of the clearing of the desk that 'Station Island' is – it is a snare that Heaney will avoid. The thrust of the poems is, in Wallace Stevens's late phrase, towards 'a new knowledge of reality'[18] and that is approached through and acknowledged by art, but is not art itself. Significantly, Sweeney is not presented as a poet, as he is habitually understood and certainly is in *At Swim-Two-Birds*. The only place he is indicated so is in Heaney's introduction to *Sweeney Astray* where one way of reading him is as 'the figure of the artist'.[19] But he is not a poet by direct indication, only he expresses himself through poems. What he allows Heaney here is distance, permits his 'signature', oddly enough, precisely by aligning with part of that same Irish tradition whose restraints he feels. What he draws attention to as an especial help to his sense of Sweeney is that he is a 'literary' creation and it is perhaps enough, in these bruising times, for Heaney to be able to take comfort from such creation in the face of numbing realities. What other purchase is there?

'In Illo Tempore', the last but one poem in the book, ends

> Now I live by a famous strand
> where seabirds cry in the small hours
> like incredible souls
>
> and even the range wall of the promenade
> that I press down on for conviction
> hardly tempts me to credit it.[20]

I have suggested that *Station Island* is in part 'clearing the desk'. It is a bookish image for what is a much wider impulse in the poetry. I used it because so much of *Station Island* is concerned with writers and writing. And the first poem in 'Sweeney Redivivus', the final part of the book, is called 'The First Gloss'. A scribe begins to write and it is a new – but now literary – 'Digging'.

> Take hold of the shaft of the pen.
> Subscribe to the first step taken
> from a justified line
> into the margin.[21]

But letters are steps and the image widens into life. And so clearing the desk – finding a space to write under all that accumulation – indicates a wider clearance. 'Clearances' is the title Heaney gives to his sequence commemorating his mother's life and death in *The Haw Lantern*[22] and the book, as a whole, is concerned to continue the clearances initiated in *Station Island*. Remember how Heaney had seen Mossbawn as giving 'a space' in 'Sunlight'? Well, in the direct and more than moving account of his mother's death in 'Clearances' he writes

> Then she was dead,
> The searching for a pulsebeat was abandoned
> And we all knew one thing by being there.
> The space we stood around had been emptied
> Into us to keep, it penetrated
> Clearances that suddenly stood open.
> High cries were felled and a pure change happened.[23]

I shall return to these words but leave them now to stand at the head of what I want to say about *The Haw Lantern*.

There is in the book a sense that Heaney has arrived somewhere, as *Station Island* had projected. He has come through. But arrival is not sensational. As the New Zealand poet, Allen Curnow, characterizes the settlement of an anticipated but unknown land, it was 'something different, something/Nobody counted on'.[24] First of all there's a good deal of allegory around. To strike another blow for New Zealand, it's a bit like penetrating the mountain ranges and finding Erewhon, an uncannily reminiscent but surreal land. 'Parable Island', 'From the Republic of Conscience', 'From the Land of the Unspoken', 'From the Canton of Expectation'; the lands are not so much geographical but mental conditions, nationality a shared state of mind, its people dispersed, but recognizing. In the land of the unspoken

> if we miss the sight of a fish
> we heard jumping and then see its ripples,
> that means one more of us is dying somewhere.[25]

These poems are 'inventions' but sometimes so palpable, the veil of allegory so thin, that they seem description, as if the world itself were vision, and fantasy. We do not translate these parables, like algebra into real numbers, but see them as intimate to our own or Heaney's condition. And so allegory is not used as a literary device, to cloak, but as a means of describing the unbelievable that exists. 'The Mud Vision' is perhaps the most palpable of these allegories.

He describes an inert world a bit like the 'casual comedy' that opens Yeats's 'Easter 1916' and which was destroyed by the events of the Rising. In it Heaney says

> we sleepwalked
> The line between panic and formulae . . .
> Watching ourselves at a distance, advantaged
> And airy as a man on a springboard
> Who keeps limbering up because the man cannot dive.

This world is vouchsafed a mud vision 'original clay, transfigured and spinning', which, as visions do, is one day gone and then forgotten. And Heaney concludes

> what might have been origin
> We dissipated in news. The clarified space
> Had retrieved neither us nor itself – except
> You could say we survived. So say that, and watch us
> Who had our chance to be mud-men, convinced and estranged,
> Figure in our own eyes for the eyes of the world.[26]

Heaney widens the terms of his own loss and exhaustion in 'Exposure' to epitomise, if not the human condition, the condition of the North, in which he is involved. In 'Hailstones' instead of mud, there is the slush that follows the melting of the sudden hail-shower. Heaney writes of the time when the shower ends as

> the truest foretaste of your aftermath –
> in that dilation
>
> when the light opened in silence
> and a car with wipers going still
> laid perfect tracks in the slush.[27]

This is our condition, still energized, our craft still finely practised, our scene the slush, not the stinging hail. But there is 'dilation', the widening of the point of vision. In what respect is it widened?

Rosemond Tuve, in her book *Allegorical Imagery*, suggests that all allegorical stories are about loss and salvation.[28] It is a remark that, if we divest it of its sense of the Last Judgement and just see it in temporal terms, could be applied more widely, and certainly to Heaney. There is judgement abroad in this book, most directly in the title-poem 'The Haw Lantern'.[29] The haw lights the winter landscape rather like the rowan did in 'Song'. Sometimes it seems like Diogenes' lantern as he seeks 'one just man'. We flinch at its judgement as it 'scans you, then moves on'. It is the ordinary condition of life 'a small light for small people' suddenly rising in judgement, testing us, whether we are just. But the poem concentrates, not on whether we are lost or saved, but on the haw itself, and its dual role as ordinary light and extraordinary judge. It is this dual possibility in creation and event that seems to me important here.

In another poem the spoonbait images the soul in life and is seen as the one drop of water that would relieve Dives' thirst, as the hero's helmet laid amidships in ritual sea-burial, and finally as a 'toy of light reeled through him upstream, snagging on nothing'.[30] The spoonbait can present these three differing 'exits' under its single appearance. What we make of our experience, of what we are shown, is, in this sense, up to us. The possibilities of the experience, are, at least, theoretically infinite, either as loss or gain. This is the width of vision then, that 'clearance' is 'space'. It recalls again his wife's remark, 'he thinks if a place is empty then he's the first there'. Death, humanly speaking, is the most palpable moment of loss and the account of Heaney's mother is paralleled by a number of obituary moments in *The Haw Lantern*, elegaic not panegyric. The muted ordinariness of death allows these moments to resume the contexts of life, 'the space we stood around had been emptied / into us to keep', and the astonished meeting at 'Number 5, New Row, Land of the Dead',

> What's this? What's this?
> And they sit down in the shining room together.[31]

It is the ancestral continuity, of course, in another guise. His mother 'taught me what her uncle once taught her', how to split coal along its grain, and Heaney writes as he opens the sequence

> Teach me now to listen,
> To strike it rich behind the linear black.[32]

The point at which *The Haw Lantern* seems to arrive, then, is one where, in a world of loss and gain, we nonetheless, cannot easily perceive what is loss and what is gain. It is a considered estimate of his experience to date and the last poem of the book 'The Riddle' – in its less frequent meaning, 'a sieve' – adumbrates the final doubt, which is, then, paradoxically an assent to the value of the experience. In its way it recalls the whole condition surrounding the imagery in *Door into the Dark*, the equivalence of the negative and the positive ways. Here is 'The Riddle':

> You never saw it used but still can hear
> The sift and fall of stuff hopped on the mesh,
>
> Clods and buds in a little dust-up,
> The dribbled pile accruing under it.
>
> Which would be better, what sticks or what falls through?
> Or does the choice itself create the value?
>
> Legs apart, deft-handed, start a mime
> to sift the sense of things from what's imagined
>
> And work out what was happening in that story
> Of the man who carried water in a riddle.
>
> Was it culpable ignorance, or was it rather
> A *via negativa* through drops and let-downs?[33]

Heaney's poetry has often rehearsed a position, declared a manifesto which he intends to put into practice, characteristically his intention to write in this way or that, for this end or that, in the knowledge of this or that pressure. He has also studied his own growth and its multiple contexts and documented them with huge power and insight. That he has grown up in Ireland and the North has made that growth more anguished than many, but his work has perhaps paid, in any case, more than its due to the Wordsworthian programme, the growth of the poet's mind. *Sweeney Astray* – translation and embodiment in another mind – has stretched his gift further. If 'Station Island' can be seen as clearing the ground to write and Sweeney a dweller n that ground, then *The Haw Lantern* comes to terms with its new contours, the lost vision, the slush, yet a world where the chaff in the sieve is itself valued. Such a realization brings his doubtful and reserved interior mind, hardly tempted to credit the appearance of the world, into consonance with his great and affirmative poetic gift and nature. Kavanagh's savage but temporary sight in *The Great Hunger*

> The hungry fiend
> Screams the apocalypse of clay
> In every corner of this land[34]

should not stalk him, however the fiends have changed their shapes since Kavanagh wrote. As Heaney himself writes in 'The Singer's House' (*Field Work*),

> when I came here first you were always singing,
> a hint of the clip of the pick
> in your winnowing climb and attack.
> Raise it again, man. We still believe what we hear.

A corollary, and perhaps a clue, to his powers of affirmation is Heaney's own writing about poetry and poets. I have tried to write this book without too much reference to the great webs of literary criticism that span everyone these days. This is in part a policy dictated by the time its readers might be supposed to have and which, I feel, is best devoted to the poems. One critic is bad enough. Two or three is a barricade. This is not to say that I am not deeply impressed by the accuracy, the sympathy and the challenge of other writers on Heaney. I have made a shortlist at the end of the book. Rather it is a matter of priorities. And if I seemed to have it in for Edna Longley this is as much to do with the vigour of her case and her thinking as it is with my sense that she is wrong. It often gives edge to your own views to examine carefully a view with which you are out of sympathy and to work out exactly why you feel that way. In the case of Edna Longley something of her passionate critical involvement informs my own reactions. It is in such a spirit – to gain passionate critical involvement – that I recommend you finally to read Heaney's criticism. I have referred a fair bit to some of the essays in *Preoccupations* (1984) already. And to close this chapter I want to point you towards *The Government of the Tongue* (1988), his second major critical collection. Heaney's criticism is never bland, but it characteristically conveys delight and renders assistance to our understanding.

At heart it attempts to clarify the procedures it observes, and this I believe to be the form of good criticism. Criticism which tries to specify what should be done as distinct from understanding what is done, is often, though not invariably, false to the governing assumptions of the art it comments on. This does not mean that it is wrong, but unless its own assumptions are as tested, then it is, at the least, at risk. For me description is to be preferred to prescription. This does not mean that criticism should have no point of view and only a power to reflect. But it does mean it is at its best when it is propelled by sympathy and understanding.

This is Heaney on Philip Larkin:

> With Larkin, we respond constantly to the melody of intelligence, to a verse that is as much commentary as it is presentation, and it is this encounter between a compassionate unfoolable mind and its own predicaments . . . that gives his poetry its first appeal. Yet while Larkin is exemplary in the way he sifts the conditions of contemporary life, refuses alibis and pushes consciousness towards an exposed condition that is neither cynicism nor despair, there survives in him a repining for a more crystalline reality to which he might give allegiance.[35]

And on Sylvia Plath:

> There is nothing *poetically* flawed about Plath's work. What may finally limit it is its dominant theme of self-discovery and self-definition, even though this concern must be understood as a valiantly, unremitting campaign against the black hole of depression and suicide. I do not suggest that the self is not the proper arena of poetry. But I believe that the greatest work occurs when a certain self-forgetfulness is attained or at least a fullness of self-possession denied to Sylvia Plath.[36]

And on poetry:

> The achievement of a poem, after all, is an experience of release. In that liberated moment, when the lyric discovers its buoyant completion and a timeless formal pleasure comes to fullness and exhaustion, something occurs which is equidistant from self-justification and self-obliteration.[37]

It is not just the intelligence and the skill of the writing but the willingness,the compulsion even, to understand both the poets and their art that makes this exemplary criticism. He does not try to reshape Larkin and Plath, to remake them in his own image. Nor does he lose his own values in theirs. Perhaps the link is the passion for the craft that they all share. But it is Heaney who observes, elucidates and gathers those passions for us. Elsewhere, and writing on the West Indian poet Dereke Walcott, he quotes Hopkins's affirmation 'that feeling, and in particular love, is the great power and spring of verse'.[38] Criticism, but not Heaney's, often misses the strength of that affirmation. If we learn that, everything follows.

Notes

Chapter 1: Introduction (pages 1–14)

1 Seamus Heaney, *Preoccupations: Selected Prose 1968–78*, London, Faber and Faber, 1980, pp. 115–30. The quotation is on p. 116.
2 Patrick Kavanagh, *Collected Poems*, London, Martin Brian & O'Keeffe, 1972, p. 136.
3 Heaney, *Preoccupations*, pp. 41–60.
4 *Ibid.*, p. 41.
5 *Ibid.*, p. 42.
6 Jonathan Swift, 'A Proposal for the Universal Use of Irish Manufacture etc.', in Herbert Davis (ed.), *Irish Tracts 1720–1723*, Oxford, Oxford University Press, 1948, p. 17. 'I heard the Archbishop of Tuam mention a pleasant Observation of some Body's: *that* Ireland *would never be happy 'till a law were made for burning every Thing that came from* England, *except their* People *and their Coals*'.
7 See Alun R. Jones, *The Life and Opinions of T. E. Hulme*, London, Victor Gollancz, 1960, pp. 23–4.
8 Heaney, *Preoccupations*, p. 55.
9 Robert Frost, *Complete Poems*, London, Cape, 1951, pp. 53–4.
10 I have in mind poems like 'Chief Petty Officer' and 'Demolition Order' (for its account of Ma Treloar). See Charles Causley, *Collected Poems 1951–1975*, London, Macmillan, 1975, pp. 26–7, pp. 149–51.
11 W. B. Yeats, *Collected Poems*, London, Macmillan, 1958, p. 204.
12 John Keats, John Barnard (ed.), *The Complete Poems*, Harmondsworth, Penguin Books, 1973, p. 431.
13 Patrick Kavanagh, *The Green Fool*, Harmondsworth, Penguin Books, 1975, p. 198.
14 Sean O'Faolain, *Stories of Sean O'Faolain*, Harmondsworth, Penguin Books, 1970, pp. 323–49.
15 *Ibid.*, pp. 336–37.
16 Philip Larkin, *The Whitsun Weddings*, London, Faber and Faber, 1964, p. 22.

Chapter 2: Nature, History, Darkness (pages 14–34)

1 Richard Kell, *The Guardian*, 3 June 1966.
2 Seamus Heaney, *Death of a Naturalist*, London, Faber and Faber, 1966, pp. 18–19. Not reprinted in *Selected Poems*.
3 Blake Morrison, *Seamus Heaney*, London, Methuen, 1982, p. 19.

4 William Wordsworth, *The Prelude* XI l. 258 (1805–6) XII l. 208 (1850). See ed. J. C. Maxwell, William Wordsworth, *The Prelude: A Parallel Text*, Harmondsworth, Penguin Books, 1971, pp. 478–79.
5 W. B. Yeats, *Collected Poems*, p. 217.
6 *Ibid.*, p. 217.
7 *Ibid.*, p. 218.
8 Edward Norman, *A History of Modern Ireland*, Harmondsworth, Penguin Books, 1971. The quotations are from p. 8 and p. 10.
9 Raymond Crotty, *Ireland in Crisis, A Study in Capitalist Colonial Undevelopment*, Dingle, Brandon, 1986.
10 W. B. Yeats, *Collected Poems*, p. 121.
11 Cecil Woodham-Smith, *The Great Hunger: Ireland 1845–9*, London, Hamish Hamilton, 1962.
12 The figures are difficult to estimate precisely but near a million, that is, one in eight of all people in the island, died, and another million emigrated.
13 Cecil Woodham-Smith, *The Great Hunger*, pp. 84–5.
14 You will find some of their stories conveniently in ed. Benedict Kiely, *The Penguin Book of Irish Short Stories*, Harmondsworth, Penguin Books, 1981.
15 Seamus Heaney, *Preoccupations*, p. 124. The lines he quotes from Yeats are in 'The Municipal Gallery Revisited', *Collected Poems*, p. 369.
16 *Ibid.*, p. 126.
17 James Joyce, *A Portrait of the Artist as a Young Man*, London, Jonathan Cape, (1916), 1956, p. 257.
18 John Keats, *Collected Poems*, p. 346. But see John Barnard's extensive note on p. 652.
19 Saint John of the Cross, *The Complete Works*, trans. and ed. E. Allison Peers, London, Burns, Oates and Washbourne, 1947, Vol. II, p. 180.
20 T. S. Eliot, *Collected Poems 1909–1962*, London, Faber and Faber, 1963, p. 64.
21 Seamus Heaney, 'The God in the Tree: Early Irish Nature Poetry', *Preoccupations*, p. 189.

Chapter 3: Image, Language, Distance (pages 34–51)

1 Seamus Heaney, *Door into the Dark*, London, Faber and Faber, 1969, p. 23.
2 Neil Corcoran, *Seamus Heaney*, London, Faber and Faber, 1986, p. 64. Corcoran refers to Christopher Ricks, *The Force of Poetry*, Oxford, 1984, where, in an essay on Andrew Marvell, Ricks notes this type of image occurring both in Marvell and Heaney.
3 Corcoran, pp. 58–9.
4 *Ibid.*, p. 60.
5 Trans. James Carney, *Medieval Irish Lyrics*, Berkeley and Los Angeles, University of California Press, 1967, pp. 22–3.
6 More information on the Irish language can be found in Douglas Hyde, *A Literary History of Ireland* (1889) new edition, with an introduction by Brian Ó Cuív, London, Ernest Benn, 1967; and in a good anthology, Seán Ó Tuama and Thomas Kinsella, *An Duanaire 1600–1900; Poems*

of the Dispossessed, Mountrath, Portlaoise, Dolmen Press, 1981. I have found Declan Kiberd's *Synge and the Irish Language*, London, Macmillan, 1979, very helpful. For the early literature, Eleanor Knott and Gerard Murphy, introduction by James Carney, *Early Irish Literature*, London, Routledge and Kegan Paul, 1966, is very good.

7 Seamus Heaney, *Station Island*, London, Faber and Faber, 1984, p. 93.
8 Seamus Heaney, *Preoccupations*, p. 45.
9 Seamus Heaney, *North*, London, Faber and Faber, 1975, p. 65.
10 Seamus Heaney, *Wintering Out*, London, Faber and Faber, 1972, dedication 'For David Hammond and Michael Longley' (page 5, unnumbered). With some variations, this is reprinted in *North* as section IV of 'Whatever You Say Say Nothing', p. 60.
11 Key books here are J. C. Beckett, *The Making of Modern Ireland 1603–1923*, London, Faber, new ed., 1981; R. F. Foster, *Modern Ireland 1600–1972*, Harmondsworth, Allen Lane, 1989; and A. T. Q. Stewart, *The Narrow Ground: aspects of Ulster, 1609–1969*, London, Faber, 1977. More general and popular, but a useful introduction is Robert Kee, *Ireland: a history*, London, Weidenfeld and Nicolson, 1980.
12 Seamus Heaney, *Preoccupations*, pp. 57–9. His source is P. V. Glob, *The Bog People*, London, Faber and Faber, 1969.
13 William Wordsworth, Preface to *Lyrical Ballads*, ed. R. L. Brett and A. R. Jones, London, Methuen, 1963, p. 260.

Chapter 4: North (pages 51–72)

1 Polly Devlin, *all of us there*, London, Weidenfeld and Nicolson, 1983, pp. 16–17.
2 *Ibid.*, Acknowledgements (page unnumbered).
3 William Carlos Williams, *Pictures from Brueghel*, (1962). Sequence printed in Charles Tomlinson (ed.), *William Carlos Williams: Selected Poems*, Harmondsworth, Penguin Books, 1976, pp. 211–21.
4 W. H. Auden, *Collected Shorter Poems 1927–1957*, London, Faber and Faber, 1966, pp. 123–4.
5 Printed in Ed. Edward Broadbridge, *Seamus Heaney*, Copenhagen, Danmarks Radio, 1977.
6 W. B. Yeats, Ed. *Oxford Book of Modern Verse*, Oxford, Clarendon Press, 1936, p. xxxiv.
7 W. B. Yeats, *Collected Poems*, p. 204.
8 Blake Morrison, *British Poetry since 1970*, Manchester, Carcanet, 1980, pp. 109–10.
9 Blake Morrison, *Seamus Heaney*, p. 68.
10 *Ibid.*, p. 66.
11 Edna Longley, *Poetry in the Wars*, Newcastle upon Tyne, Bloodaxe Books, 1986, p. 154.
12 *Ibid.*, p. 141.
13 *Ibid.*, p. 185.
14 W. B. Yeats, *Collected Poems*, p. 204.
15 Edna Longley, *Poetry in the Wars*, p. 200.
16 W. B. Yeats, *Collected Poems*, p. 217.

17 The epigraphs are not given in *Selected Poems* so I'll print them here.

Fair seedtime had my soul, and I grew up
Fostered alike by beauty and by fear;
Much favoured in my birthplace, and no less
In that beloved Vale to which, erelong,
I was transplanted . . .

(William Wordsworth: *The Prelude*)

He [the stable-boy] had a book of Orange rhymes, and the days when we read them together in the hay-loft gave me the pleasure of rhyme for the first time. Later on I can remember being told, when there was a rumour of a Fenian rising, that rifles were being handed out to the Orangemen; and presently, when I began to dream of my future life, I thought I would like to die fighting the Fenians.

(W. B. Yeats: *Autobiographies*)

18 Graham Greene, *The Ministry of Fear*, London, Heinemann, 1950.
19 *Ibid.*, p. 140.
20 *Ibid.*, p. 267.
21 *Ibid.*, p. 268.
22 Seamus Heaney, *The Government of the Tongue*, London, Faber and Faber, 1988, pp. xi–xxiii.

Chapter 5: Field Work (pages 72–88)

1 Blake Morrison, and Andrew Motion (eds), *Penguin Book of Contemporary British Poetry (PBCBP)*, Harmondsworth, Penguin Books, 1982.
2 Seamus Heaney, *Field Work*, London, Faber and Faber, 1979, p. 12.
3 *Ibid.*, pp. 21–4. *PBCBP* pp. 33–5.
4 Seamus Heaney, *An Open Letter*, Derry, Field Day Theatre Company, 1983, p. 9.
5 Seamus Heaney, *Field Work*, p. 56.
6 *Ibid.*, p. 58, *PBCBP*, p. 36.
7 *Ibid.*, pp. 29–30.
8 *Ibid.*, p. 28.
9 *Ibid.*, p. 27.
10 *Ibid.*, p. 43.
11 *Ibid.*, pp. 25–6.
12 T. S. Eliot, *Collected Poems*, London, Faber and Faber, p. 39.
13 Seamus Heaney, *Field Work*, p. 44.
14 Samuel Taylor Coleridge, E. H. Coleridge (ed.), *Poetical Works*, Oxford, Oxford University Press, 1978, pp. 178–81.
15 W. B. Yeats, *Collected Poems*, pp. 148–52.
16 Seamus Heaney, *Field Work*, pp. 31–2.
17 *Ibid.*, p. 11.
18 *Ibid.*, pp. 59–60.
19 *Ibid.*, p. 13.
20 Adrienne Rich, *The Fact of a Doorframe: Poems Selected and New 1950–1984*, New York, W. W. Norton, 1984, p. 56. 'In the Woods'.

Chapter 6: Station Island and After (pages 88–102)

1 Seamus Heaney, *Station Island*, London, Faber and Faber, 1984.
2 Georges Charbonnier, *Conversations with Claude Lévi-Strauss*, London, 1969, p. 127.
3 Seamus Heaney, *Station Island*, 'Away from it All', p. 17.
4 *Ibid*., p. 20.
5 *Ibid*., pp. 18–19.
6 *Ibid*., p. 27.
7 T. S. Eliot, 'The Three Voices of Poetry', in *On Poetry and Poets*, London, Faber and Faber, 1957, p. 89.
8 Seamus Heaney, *Station Island*, pp. 56–8.
9 Flann O'Brien, *At Swim-Two-Birds*, Harmondsworth, Penguin Books, 1967, p. 85.
10 Seamus Heaney, *Station Island*, 'The King of the Ditchbacks' II, p. 57.
11 W. H. Auden, *The Dyer's Hand*, London, Faber and Faber, 1963, 'The Poet and the City', p. 77.
12 Seamus Heaney 'The King of the Ditchbacks', pp. 57–8.
13 William Carleton, 'The Lough Derg Pilgrim' (1829); Denis Devlin, 'Lough Derg' (1946); Patrick Kavanagh, 'Lough Derg' (written 1942); Sean O'Faolain 'Lovers of the Lake'. I have written more fully on this theme in 'Sean O'Faolain's "Lovers of the Lake"' in *Journal of the Short Story in English*, University of Angers, no. 8, Spring 1987, pp. 59–69.
14 Not in Kavanagh's *Collected Poems* but easily available in ed. Brendan Kennelly, *The Penguin Book of Irish Verse*, Harmondsworth, Penguin Books, 2nd ed., 1981, pp. 344–62.
15 Paul Durcan in his foreword to Patrick Kavanagh, *Lough Derg*, London, Martin Brian & O'Keeffe, 1978.
16 On Station Island stone circles, believed to be the remaining foundations of ancient monastic cells, are called 'beds'. In certain religious ceremonies (e.g. the Stations of the Cross) a 'station' is a place where you say prayers, usually involving a set form or sequence. At the 'stations' on Station Island, you walk around the stone circle, barefoot, and pray at each of the 'beds' of stone. Heaney's own note is on p. 122 of *Station Island*.
17 *King Lear*, V, iii, 309.
18 Wallace Stevens, 'Not Ideas about the Thing but The Thing Itself', in Holly Stevens (ed.), *The Palm at the End of the Mind*, New York, Vintage Books, 1972, pp. 387–8.
19 Seamus Heaney, *Sweeney Astray*, London, Faber and Faber, 1984, second page of introduction, unnumbered.
20 Seamus Heaney, *Station Island*, p. 118.
21 *Ibid*., p. 97.
22 Seamus Heaney, *The Haw Lantern*, London, Faber and Faber, 1987, pp. 24–32.
23 *Ibid*., p. 31.
24 Allen Curnow, 'The Unhistoric Story', in Vincent O'Sullivan (ed.), *An Anthology of Twentieth Century New Zealand Poetry*, second ed., Oxford, Oxford University Press, 1976, pp. 116–17.

25 Seamus Heaney, *The Haw Lantern*, 'From the Land of the Unspoken', p. 19.
26 *Ibid.*, pp. 48–9.
27 *Ibid.*, p. 35.
28 Rosemond Tuve, *Allegorical Imagery, Some Medieval Books and Their Posterity*, Princeton, Princeton University Press, 1966, p. 28.
29 Seamus Heaney, *The Haw Lantern*, p. 7.
30 *Ibid.*, p. 21.
31 *Ibid.*, p. 26.
32 *Ibid.*, p. 24.
33 *Ibid.*, p. 51.
34 Patrick Kavanagh, *Collected Poems*, p. 55.
35 Seamus Heaney, *The Government of the Tongue*, pp. 15–16.
36 *Ibid.*, p. 168.
37 *Ibid.*, p. xxii.
38 *Ibid.*, p. 27.

Suggestions for Further Reading

Seamus Heaney's major collections of poetry to date are:

Death of a Naturalist, London, Faber and Faber, 1966.
Door into the Dark, London, Faber and Faber, 1969.
Wintering Out, London, Faber and Faber, 1972.
North, London, Faber and Faber, 1975.
Field Work, London, Faber and Faber, 1979.
Selected Poems 1965–1975, London, Faber and Faber, 1980.
Sweeney Astray, Derry, Field Day, 1983: London, Faber and Faber, 1984.
Station Island, London, Faber and Faber, 1984.
The Haw Lantern, London, Faber and Faber, 1987.

Some of these poems are also available in Blake Morrison and Andrew Motion (eds.) *The Penguin Book of Contemporary British Poetry*, Hardmondsworth, Penguin Books, 1982.

'An Open Letter', Heaney's response to the appearance of his poems in an anthology of British poetry is available in *Ireland's Field Day*, London, Hutchinson, 1985.

His two major collections of prose writings are:

Preoccupations: Selected Prose, 1968–1978, London, Faber and Faber, 1980.
The Government of the Tongue, London, Faber and Faber, 1988.

Of the several critical books about his work, I have found the following particularly useful:

Blake Morrison, *Seamus Heaney*, London, Methuen, 1982, particularly strong on Heaney's relationship with English Romanticism and what Morrison calls 'the mainstream of English poetry'.
Tony Curtis (ed.), *The Art of Seamus Heaney*, Bridgend, Poetry Wales Press, second ed., 1985, includes an interesting essay on *Wintering Out* by Philip Hobsbaum and the manuscript drafts of 'North'.
Neil Corcoran, *Seamus Heaney*, London, Faber and Faber, 1986, contains a good deal of biographical material and pertinent analyses of the poems.

Two more general books with material bearing on Heaney's work are:

Seamus Deane, *Celtic Revival*, London, Faber and Faber, 1985

Edna Longley, *Poetry in the Wars*, Newcastle upon Tyne, Bloodaxe Books, 1984.

Polly Devlin in *all of us there*, London, Weidenfeld and Nicolson, 1983, includes incidental information about Heaney's early background.

The importance of the Irish context in reading Heaney's work cannot be too emphatically underlined. As well as the titles listed in notes 6 and 11 for Chapter Two, you could turn to:

Literature

Ireland's Field Day, London, Hutchinson, 1985, includes some valuable essays on the Irish contexts.

Seamus Deane, *A Short History of Irish Literature*, London, Hutchinson, 1984, the best general study available.

Robert Hogan (ed.), *The Macmillan Dictionary of Irish Literature*, London, Macmillan, 1980, an extremely good work of reference.

Roger McHugh and Maurice Harmon, *Short History of Anglo-Irish Literature*, Totowa, New Jersey, Barnes and Noble, 1982, very thorough.

Tom Paulin, *Ireland and the English Crisis*, Newcastle upon Tyne, Bloodaxe Books, 1984, forceful and intelligent.

Archaeology

Seán P. O. Ríordáin, *Antiquities of the Irish Countryside*, London, Methuen, third ed., 1953.

Peter Harbison, *The Archaeology of Ireland*, London, The Bodley Head, 1974.

Anthologies

Maurice Harmon (ed.), *Irish Poetry after Yeats*, Portmarnock, County Dublin, Wolfhound Press, 1979.

Brendan Kennelly (ed.), *The Penguin Book of Irish Verse*, Harmondsworth, Penguin Books, second ed., 1981.

Paul Muldoon (ed.), *The Faber Book of Contemporary Irish Poetry*, London, Faber and Faber, 1986.

General Culture

Brian de Breffny (ed.), *The Irish World: The History and Cultural Achievement of the Irish People*, London, Thames and Hudson, 1977, substantial and useful.

Tim Pat Coogan (ed.), *Ireland and the Arts*, London, Namara Press, n.d. A *Literary Review* Special Issue, a wide-ranging compilation.

James Plunkett, *The Gems She Wore*, London, Hutchinson, 1972.

Jeanne Sheehy, *The Rediscovery of Ireland's Past: The Celtic Revival 1830–1930*, London, Thames and Hudson, 1980, mainly the visual arts.

William Trevor, *A Writer's Ireland*, New York, Viking, 1984, the impact of landscape on literature.

Index

Aarhus, 47, 48
Antrim, County, 37, 38
Armagh, County, 37
Armstrong, Sean, 77
Auden, W. H., 53, 92
  'Musée des Beaux Arts', 53

Bann, River, 37
Bellaghy, 1
Bible, the, 4, 11, 12, 23, 31
Bloody Sunday, 75, 76
Bogside, 75, 76
Boyne, River, 55
Brueghel, 53–4
Buile Suibhne, 91

California, 50
Calvinism, 11
Canada, 7
Carleton, William, 93, 94–5
  Lough Derg Pilgrim, 94
Carlingford Lough, 56
Carney, James, 41
Causley, Charles, 10, 13–14, 103
Chaucer, Geoffrey, 69
Coleridge, Samuel Taylor, 84
  'This Lime Tree Bower my Prison', 84
Corcoran, Neil, 35, 39
Crotty, Raymond, 18
Curnow, Allen, 98, 107

Dante, 95
Dardanelles, 87
Deane, Seamus, 67, 68
Denmark, 47ff, 58
Derg, Lough, 12, 93ff
Derry city, 75
Derry, County, 1, 37, 64
Devlin, Denis, 93
Devlin, Polly, 52–3
Dingle Peninsula, 32
Dombrain, Sir James, 19–22
Donegal, County, 50, 93
Donnelly, Brian, 54
Down, County, 37
Dublin, 55, 91
Durcan, Paul, 93
'Dying Gaul, The', 61

Easter Rising (1916), The, 27, 57, 63, 98
Eliot, T. S., 31, 82, 91, 92
  'Gerontion', 82
  The Waste Land, 31, 92

Famine, Great (1845–9), The, 18ff, 26, 27
First World War, 56, 87
Frost, Robert, 10
  'Mending Wall', 10

Gallarus Oratory, 31–4
Glanmore, 85–6, 90
Glasgow, 91
Glob, P. V., 48
Greene, Grahame, 70
  The Ministry of Fear, 70
Guardian, The, 14
Gunnar, 56

Hardy, Thomas, 27
Heaney, Margaret, 97–8, 100
Heaney, Marie, 52–3, 83, 99–100
Heaney, Mary, 51–2
Heaney, Patrick, 2–3, 79
Heaney, Seamus (poetry)
  Death of a Naturalist (1966), 1, 14, 15, 18
    'An Advancement of Learning', 15

Heaney, Seamus (poetry) – *cont.*
'At a Potato Digging', 18, 24–7, 49
'The Barn', 33
'Blackberry-Picking', 15
'Churning Day', 15
'Death of a Naturalist', 16–17, 26
'Digging', 1–5, 6, 7, 8, 9, 10, 13, 14, 15, 16, 17, 24, 26, 27, 36, 49, 97
'The Diviner', 14
'Follower', 14, 79
'For the Commander of the *Eliza*', 18–24, 26
'Lovers on Aran', 14
'Personal Helicon', 15, 33
Door into the Dark (1969), 5, 8, 14, 15, 27, 31, 33, 34, 35, 38, 40, 51, 94, 100
'At Ardboe Point', 35–6
'Bogland', 5–9, 10, 13, 14, 27, 31, 49
'The Forge', 27–34
'Girls Bathing, Galway, 1965', 35, 36
'A Lough Neagh Sequence', 37, 38ff, 58
'Lifting', 38
'Up the Shore', 38, 39
'Vision', 38, 39
'In Gallarus Oratory', 31–4
'The Peninsula', 33
'The Plantation', 37, 38
'Requiem for the Croppies', 27
'Shoreline', 14, 35
'Undine', 36, 38, 51
'The Wife's Tale', 34
Wintering Out (1972), 9, 40, 44, 45, 51, 78, 94
'Anahorish', 40–2, 51
'Bog Oak', 44, 45
'Broagh', 41
'Bye-Child', 49–50, 94
dedicatory poem to *Wintering Out*, 44, 45, 105
'Gifts of Rain', 44, 78
'Goodnight', 51
'Limbo', 51, 94
'Maighdean Mara', 51
'A New Song', 44
'Oracle', 44
'The Other Side', 9–13, 67
'Servant Boy', 44, 46
'The Tollund Man', 46–9, 51, 54, 58, 62
'Traditions', 40, 41, 42–4, 61
'Westering', 50, 94
North (1975), 43, 51–72, 90, 92
'Act of Union', 62, 63
'Funeral Rites', 55–7, 69
'The Grauballe Man', 58–61, 66, 72
'Kinship', 62, 63–4
'Mossbawn', 86
'The Seed Cutters', 51, 53–4, 71
'Sunlight', 51–3, 71, 98
'North', 57–8
'Punishment', 61, 63
'Singing School', 65–72
'A Constable Calls', 65, 66–7, 69
'Exposure', 68, 71–3, 86, 99
'Fosterage', 67, 68
'Ministry of Fear', 43–4, 65, 67, 68, 69–70
'Orange Drums, Tyrone, 1966', 65
'Summer 1969', 68
'Viking Dublin: Trial Pieces', 70–1
'Whatever You Say Say Nothing', 105
Field Work (1979), 72–88, 89, 95, 101
'An Afterwards', 83
'The Badgers', 73, 81–3
'Casualty', 75–7, 83
'Elegy', 84
'Glanmore Sonnets', 73, 84–6, 88
'The Guttural Muse', 80
'The Harvest Bow', 78–80, 83
'In Memoriam Francis Ledwidge', 87
'In Memoriam Sean O'Riada', 80
'Oysters', 86–7
'A Postcard from North Antrim', 77, 84
'September Song', 80, 84
'The Singer's House', 80, 101
'Song', 77–8, 83, 99

'The Strand at Lough Beg', 95
'Triptych', 73, 87
'After a Killing', 73–5, 83
'Sibyl', 73, 87
An Open Letter (1983), 75
Sweeney Astray (1983), 88, 91, 92, 97, 101
Station Island (1984), 88–97, 98
'Chekhov on Sakhalin', 90–1, 96
'The King of the Ditchbacks', 91–2
'A Migration', 91, 96
'Sandstone Keepsake', 90
'Station Island', 12, 42, 69, 88, 91, 92–7, 101
'Sweeney Redivivus', 91, 97
'The First Gloss', 97
'In Illo Tempore', 97
The Haw Lantern (1987), 88, 97–101
'Clearances', 97–8, 100
'From the Canton of Expectation', 98
'From the Land of the Unspoken', 98
'From the Republic of Conscience', 98
'Hailstones', 99
'The Haw Lantern', 99
'The Mud Vision', 98–9
'Parable Island', 98
'The Spoonbait', 99
'The Riddle', 100
Heaney, Seamus (prose)
The Government of the Tongue (1988), 72, 88, 101–2
'The Interesting Case of Nero, Chekhov's Cognac and a Knocker', 72
Preoccupations (1980), 24, 27, 32, 34, 42, 48, 101
'Englands of the Mind', 34
'Feeling into Words', 5, 8, 14, 42, 48
'From Monaghan to the Grand Canal', 4, 24–5, 26–7
'The God in the Tree', 32–4
'In the Country of Convention', 34
Heraclitus, 59
Homer, 27
Hopkins, Gerard Manley, 42, 67, 68, 69, 102
Hughes, Ted, 23
Hulme, T. E., 7

Irish Free State, 45, 74
IRA, 75, 76
Irish Rebellion (1798), 18, 27

Jews, the, 11
Joyce, James, 3, 28, 42, 43, 49, 67, 68, 73, 93, 94, 96
Finnegan's Wake, 96
Portrait of the Artist as a Young Man, 3, 28, 68, 96
Ulysses, 43, 96
Jutland, 47, 49

Kafka, Franz, 38
Kavanagh, Patrick, 4, 12, 13, 24–5, 26–7, 67, 68, 93, 94, 101
'Epic', 4
The Great Hunger, 4, 24–5, 26–7, 101
The Green Fool, 4, 12
Lough Derg, 93
Tarry Flynn, 4
Keats, John, 12, 29
Lamia, 12
'The Ode on a Grecian Urn', 29
Kell, Richard, 14
Kerry, County, 32

Larkin, Philip, 13, 14, 102
'The Whitsun Weddings', 13
Lawrence, D. H., 3, 14
Sons and Lovers, 3
Ledwidge, Francis, 87
Lévi-Strauss, Claude, 90
Longley, Edna, 62–5, 101
Lorca, Federico García, 67
Lowell, Robert, 84, 92
Imitations, 92

McCartney, Colum, 95
McLaverty, Michael, 67, 68
Mansfield, Katherine, 67, 68
Meath, County, 56
Megacerous Hibernicus, 6
Milton, John, 23
Monaghan, County, 4
Morrison, Blake, 15, 61–2

Mossbawn, 1, 98
Mucker, 4

National Front, 65
Neagh, Lough, 37–9
Newgrange, 56
Norman, Edward, 18

O'Brien, Flann, 91–2
  At Swim-Two-Birds, 92, 97
O'Connor, Frank, 23
O'Faolain, Sean, 12, 23, 93
  'Lovers of the Lake', 12
O'Flaherty, Liam, 23
Orange Order, 65
O'Riada, Sean, 80
Orwell, George, 14, 70
  1984, 14, 70
Owen, Wilfred, 56

Parachute Regiment, 75
Peel, Sir Robert, 19
Penguin Book of Contemporary British Poetry, 72, 75, 84
Pinter, Harold, 38
Plath, Sylvia, 102
Pope, Alexander, 23, 68
  The Dunciad, 68
Portstewart, 87
Protestant Telegraph, The, 64

Queen's University, Belfast, 8

Rich, Adrienne, 87–8, 106
Ricks, Christopher, 35
Routh, Sir Randolph, 19
Royal Society of Literature, 5

St John of the Cross, 30, 94
  Spiritual Canticle, 30
St Patrick's Purgatory, 93
Sakhalin, 90
Sargasso Sea, 38
Scandinavia, 55ff, 58
Shakespeare, William, 31, 43, 95
  Henry V, 43
  King Lear, 95
  'Sonnet 130', 31
Spenser, Edmund, 46
  The Faerie Queene, 46
  View of the Present State of Ireland, 46
Station Island (place), 93
Stevens, Wallace, 97, 107
Strangford Lough, 56
Sweeney (Irish king), 91–2, 97
Swift, Jonathan, 7, 103

Tacitus, 63
Tamniarn, 1
Times, The, 54
Toomebridge, 37, 38
Trevelyan, Charles Edward, 19, 21
Tuve, Rosemond, 99

Ulster, 45
Ulster Orchestra, 80

Vikings, 41, 55ff, 90
Volsungsaga, 56

Walcott, Derek, 23, 102
Westerns, 8
Westminster, 64
Whitman, Walt, 8
Wicklow, County, 49, 71, 73, 83, 85, 86, 91
William of Orange, 65
Williams, William Carlos, 53
  'Pictures from Brueghel', 53
Woodham-Smith, Cecil, 18–23
Wordsworth, William, 15, 16, 49, 67, 68, 69, 101, 106
  The Prelude, 15, 68, 69

Yeats, W. B., 7, 11, 17, 18, 24–5, 56–7, 63, 65, 67, 68, 76, 84, 98, 106
  'Easter 1916', 11, 57, 63, 76, 98
  'In Memory of Major Robert Gregory', 84
  'The Municipal Gallery Revisited', 68
  Oxford Book of Modern Verse (1936), 56
  'Sailing to Byzantium', 17, 65
  'September 1913', 18
Ypres, 87